Summer 2017!

"With the complete exposure of the head, a veritable orgy is invited. Either in its natural state or with its embellishments of makeup, jewels, or elaborate hairdos, nothing can restrain the imagination from the most riotous speculations."

Man Ray

MICK ROCK
EXPOSED

THE FACES OF ROCK 'N' ROLL

FOREWORD BY **TOM STOPPARD**
AFTERWORD BY **ANDREW LOOG OLDHAM**

CHRONICLE BOOKS

SAN FRANCISCO

This book is for Joan, who was there at the very beginning.

Library of Congress Cataloging-in-Publication Data available.

ISBN: 978-0-8118-7136-5

Created and produced for Chronicle Books by
Palazzo Editions Limited
2 Wood Street,
Bath, BA1 2JQ,
United Kingdom

Publisher: Colin Webb

Art Director: Adrian Cross

All photos remastered by Lucky Singh of Lucky Digital Inc, NYC
www.luckydigital.us

Manufactured in Singapore.

10 9 8 7 6 5 4 3 2 1

Chronicle Books LLC
680 Second Street
San Francisco, California 94107

www.chroniclebooks.com

FOREWORD

Syd Barrett brought us together. That was getting on for forty years after Mick photographed him for the album cover of *The Madcap Laughs*. I love rock 'n' roll but I'm not a rock 'n' roll nerd, and I didn't know who had shot those photos until I was writing my own *Rock 'n' Roll* and reading up about Syd, whom I'd put into my play. In Tim Willis's book about Syd Barrett (*Madcap*, 2002) I read: "Mick Rock was commissioned to take a photograph, and turned up at Earls Court Square to discover that Barrett had piled his mattress and a few possessions against the wall and painted the dusty, un-primed floorboards alternately blue and orange. . . . Rock fitted a wide lens and, from a single roll of film, captured one of the coolest album sleeves of all time."

And so it came to pass, I was visiting San Francisco from New York, staying as usual in a hotel on Geary right opposite the S.F. Art Exchange, a gallery that makes something of a speciality of rock stars. I'd just missed a Mick Rock show, but there were a few photos left over, including some from the Earls Court Square shoot. I bought two of them and had the gallery ship the pictures (the fact that *ship* is the transitive verb still used for *fly* is worth a parenthesis; so anyway, I had the gallery *ship*) to my hotel in New York, where in due course they arrived shortly after I got back there, shortly after which I saw the same Syd/Mick photos, a little cheaper as I recall, in the window of a gallery round the corner from my hotel, but it's only rock 'n' roll. I gave one of my photos away as a present and *shipped* the second one to London, where I live and look at Syd-by-Mick every day because it hangs opposite where I eat.

So then I called Mick (the gallery told me he lived in New York) and invited Mick to *Rock 'n' Roll*. That's when I found out he looked like someone who'd changed his name to Mick Rock. *Mick Rock!* Photographer to rock royalty, you couldn't not make it up, but Mick apparently didn't, he's not cheesy, he's cool, is Mick Rock. He looked a little like the Czech rock-lover in the play, tall, dark, and romantic, and he came to the play with his wife, Pati, who looked a lot like the hippie English single mum who loves the one who looks a little like Mick. And Mick and Pati came with the actors who looked like them, and actors who didn't, to the Bar Centrale where we all asked him questions because Mick *had been* there and we were only pretending. We were all quietly excited. Mick doesn't really do excitement quietly. I think he took some photos. When the actress who looked like Pati went home, a woman came to the table and said to Pati, "You were wonderful in the play." It made sense to me.

Tom Stoppard

INTRODUCTION

"Anything is possible if the mind is flexible enough, whether that flexibility is the result of wisdom or madness." Tristan Corbière, 1873

Photography happened to me. It idly drifted into my life, set up shop, and took over. I was studying modern languages and literature at Cambridge University and my imagination was filled to the brim with the works and exploits of great literary figures, especially of certain chemically inspired poets and writers such as the Symbolists Rimbaud, Baudelaire, and Nerval; the Romantics Byron, Shelley, and Coleridge; and the Beats Kerouac, Ginsberg, and Burroughs. I had aspirations, but they tended toward literary glory and a bohemian lifestyle.

Then one balmy afternoon in the fall of 1968, in a state of extreme inebriation, I picked up a friend's camera and started that click click thing, aimed at a young, blonde lady friend. A few days later, in that same friend's room, I remembered the camera and the clicking. He told me there hadn't been any film in the camera for months. He was born into a family of substance and the camera was just another toy that he had rarely used.

The issue of those images, forever lost, piqued my curiosity. So I bought a single roll of film, had my friend carefully load the camera, primed my charged instrument, and—in a similar state of out-of-body consciousness—spent some more time with the same young lady. And so began the magical dance of shutter, light, and subject. Somewhere, I still harbor those first exposures. . . .

Since I was an arts student, I had experimental time on my hands. So I dabbled some more, snapped at girlfriends, male friends, and their girlfriends. I even learned how to load my own film, process it, and make my own prints. I had to, as I barely had enough money to pay for the raw film. Soon there were further opportunities. In those days of the emerging UK underground scene, where students and the hip artists of the time mingled freely, I became friendly with some local rock 'n' rollers. In many ways the name was my entrée. They all wanted to know if it was given, or manufactured. The fact that it was reflected in my birth certificate only added to my cachet.

I had met Syd Barrett through some mutual friends. He had grown up in Cambridge, and when I came into his orbit (Christmas 1966) he was the lead man of Pink Floyd, a virtually unknown act at the time. By the fall of 1969, Syd was several months gone from what had become the most significant act of the London psychedelic rock scene and I owned my first camera (albeit secondhand and severely battered). Syd, with whom I had become a hangout pal, suggested I aim my clicks at him. I still had decidedly literary aspirations, but was enjoying the nonintellectual inner process that my camera had opened up for me. I felt no pressure to produce anything of significance—to me it was just playing with a friend, so I had a freeflowing mind that magical afternoon of our first session. He was the perfect subject for me. He had the aura and the look of the *poète maudit*, extolled by nineteenth-century French Symbolist writers. And that's what comes through so strongly in the resultant images. It was the first time I truly channeled "resonance" through a photographic lens. I didn't really understand what had happened, but my level of excitement grew, and it left a distinctly unique impression in my imagination. I had sampled the "alchemical moment," and it focused my emerging sensibilities.

For a while, I had a few articles and interviews published. Sometimes I provided photos to illustrate these pieces (and to make a little extra cash). But in some strange and seductive way, the lens strengthened its hold on my energies to such a degree that I no longer had time for the way of the pen. I found that my photos could do all the talking for me. It became apparent that they spoke far louder than any of my words.

In recent times, I have often been asked what inspired me to become such an unrepentant slave to the camera, and I have one clear answer: the extreme good fortune I had in exposing the unique charisma of many of my early subjects. I had come out of a decidedly non-visual background and education and knew little of the names and work of other photographers. Without these rock 'n' rollers, I would not have developed as an image man. Of course, later in the seventies, I discovered the work of Man Ray, George Hurrell, Horst B. Horst, Irving Penn, and Helmut Newton, and they did inspire me.

A key moment in my exploration of the world of imagery was my encounter with David Bowie in early March 1972 (which I have written about at length in articles and other books). His public persona had just morphed into its revolutionary alter ego, Ziggy Stardust. At this time, he was still essentially an "underground" figure. *Ziggy Stardust*, his massively successful breakout album, would not be released for another three months. He was, in truth, a photographer's dream, although no other lensman realized it at the time. Of course, a few short months later, every shutterbug out there wanted a piece of his image. God bless Ziggy Bowie!! I certainly give myself credit for intuitive foresight. I give David credit for everything else!

My relationship with David opened up all kinds of new doors (Lou Reed, Iggy & the Stooges, Mott the Hoople, and the great mime artist Lindsay Kemp, who mentored David in the wiles of stagecraft and presentation). Throughout the seventies, many people referred to me as Bowie's personal photographer, such was the power of his shadow. Other than a few performance photos, however, it would be many years before we again created photographic alchemy. (Check out the cover of this book, one of my all-time fave frames.) This kind of mythology is hard to fracture when it becomes embedded in the general consciousness. At the time of my first book, *A Photographic Record 1969–1980* (published in 1995), I was dubbed "The Man Who Shot the Seventies," which seems to have stuck, although I'm really not sure what it means!

And so it continued. Along came Queen, Roxy Music, Rocky Horror, New York Dolls, Sex Pistols, Ramones, Dead Boys, Siouxsie, Talking Heads, Joan Jett, etc. For several years I was obsessed with the London/New York connection, checking out my inner demons, savoring the freedom of movement between the twin capitals of post-modern rock/underground culture, swimming in the experimental delights available to those whose curiosity far outflanked their intelligence.

Eventually my love affair with New York overwhelmed me, and I completely lost myself in that fantasy of "living on the edge 24 hours a day": a very unfortunate trap, in which, of course, I had considerable company. I could list a bevy of broken lives and corpses to underscore this (a number are featured in this book). However, in this period all was not wasted (although I certainly was). I produced a large body of experimental photography and tumbled into a new obsession, my photoart. I found that I love to bend my photographs into new visual forms. Occasionally, I've dragged one or two of these reconfigured images out of the closet (an example is included in this book). At some point in the not-too-distant future, I intend to parade them in greater numbers.

The trough I had so relentlessly plummeted into had blinded me to many essential considerations in the art of survival. In the long winter of 1996, I almost died and had to undergo heart bypass surgery. My life at that moment provided a very bleak picture: I was a victim of my own wayward imagination. Fortunately, as friends have been known to opine, in many ways I was born under a very lucky star, and the gory details of that unfortunate period need not be indulged here.

In fact this near-death experience proved to be a blessing, thanks to certain generous souls who saved my life (and who are fully credited at the end of this tome). My illness cleared all the self-indulgent cobwebs and romantic misconceptions out of my psyche and allowed me to be reborn. Large doses of Kundalini yoga and massage provided me with a clear vision that enabled me to claw my way back to the culture of the here and now, which is where I feel most comfortable. We have now entered a truly golden age of photography, and I'm absolutely grateful to be a part of it.

The past still swirls around my reconditioned antennae. The demand for books, exhibitions, and licensing have informed and polished my reputation in recent years and opened up the doors to an endless stream of nouveau rockers, a good number of whom have found their way into this collection. I include in that description the delightful Kate Moss; the uniquely talented moviemaker John Cameron Mitchell, creator of the renegade musical *Hedwig and the Angry Inch*; the brilliantly innovative choreographer Michael Clark; and my friend Kanzaburo Nakamura, Japan's most acclaimed Kabuki Theatre Master. . . . It is here that I find my greatest excitement.

I love the camera and its magical reflections. In many ways I love it more than ever: maybe because I so nearly completely lost it. I love the access it gives me to an endless stream of imagery. I love the whole process involved in a session: gathering the elements, stirring the juices, finding the focus, building the energy, exploring and expanding all the possibilities within each individual circumstance. It charges my batteries like nothing else. Something happens inside of me—a kind of transformation. I enter the magic garden of the frame. I become the other, the image-maker, and everything is possible. It's intensely therapeutic.

This is what I love to do above all. . . .

Mick Rock

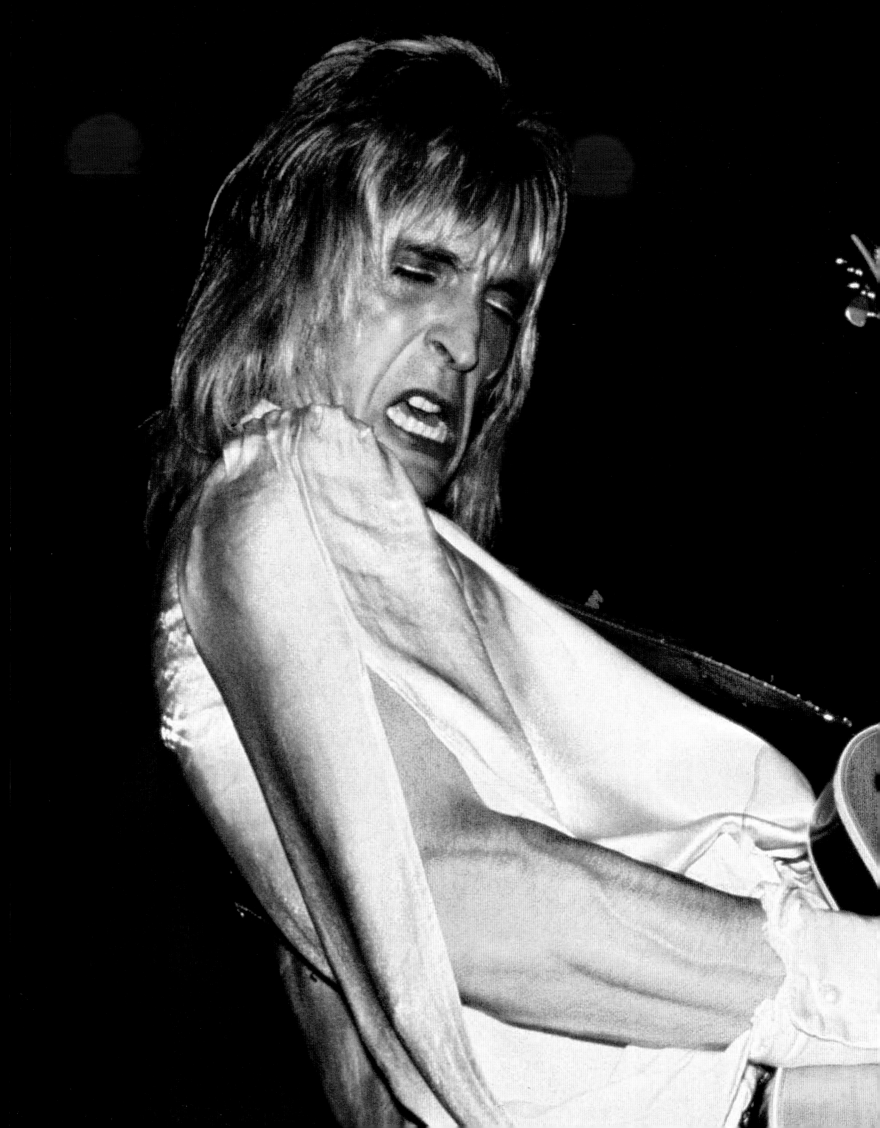

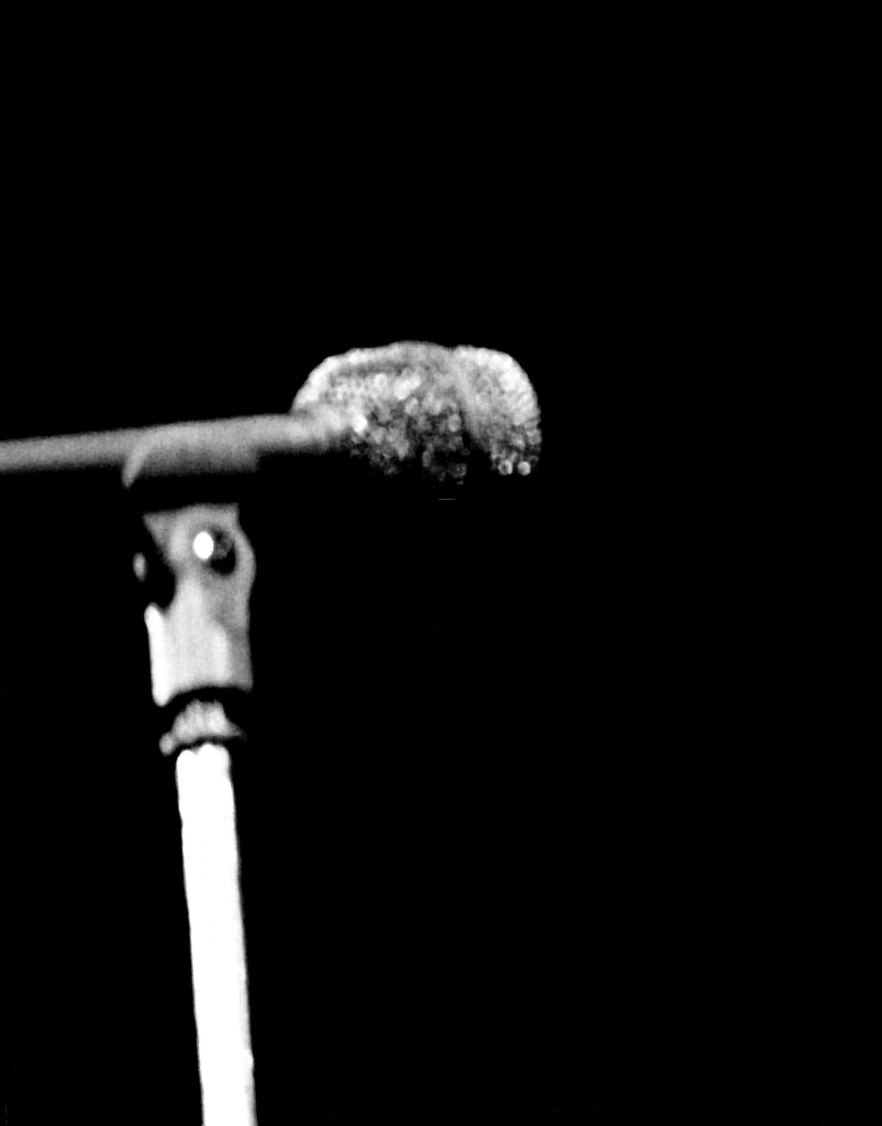

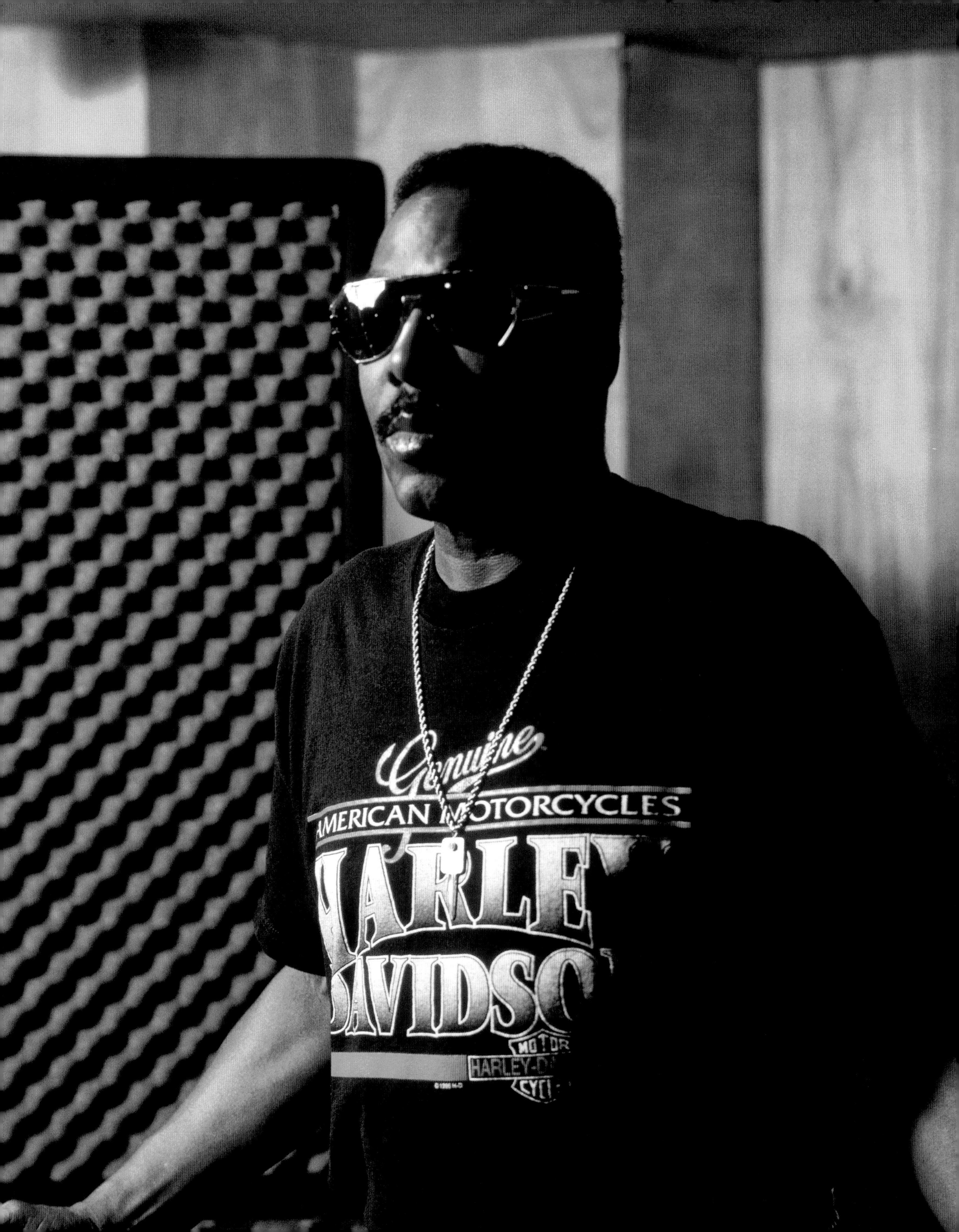
Genuine
AMERICAN MOTORCYCLES

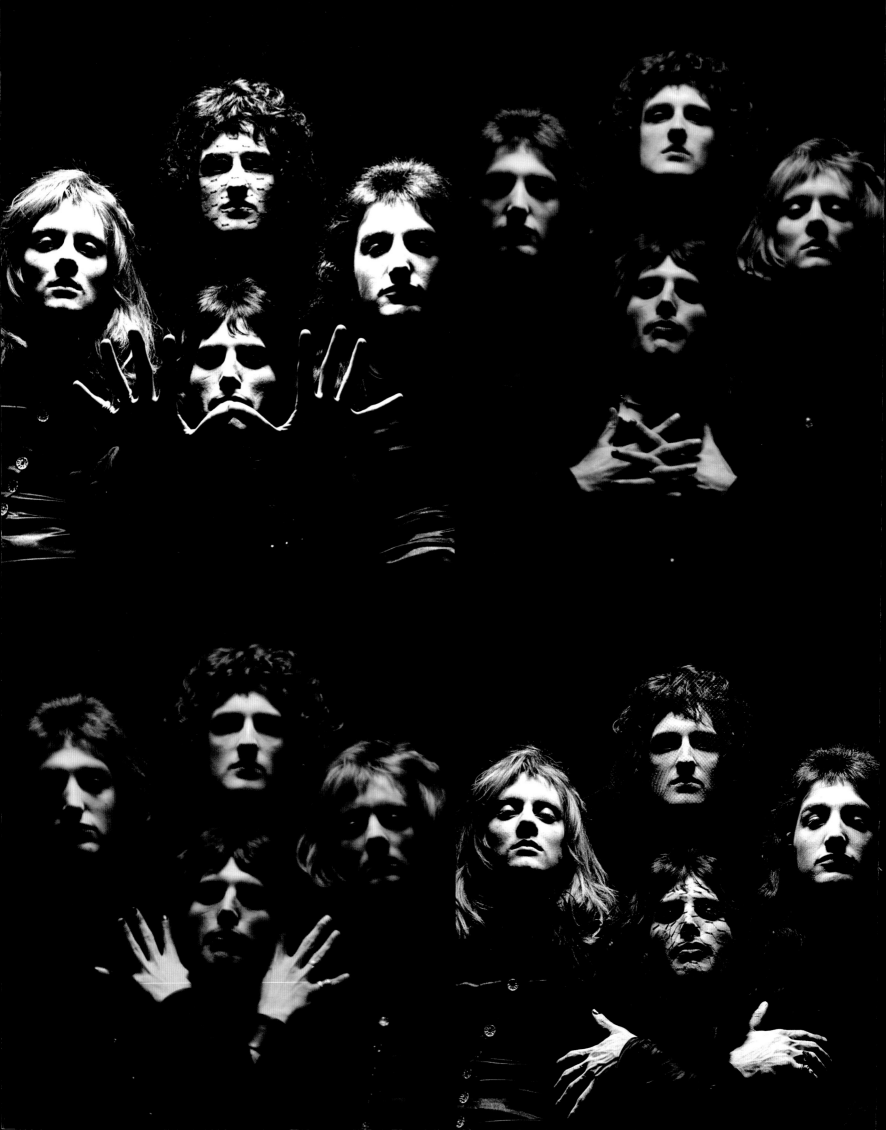

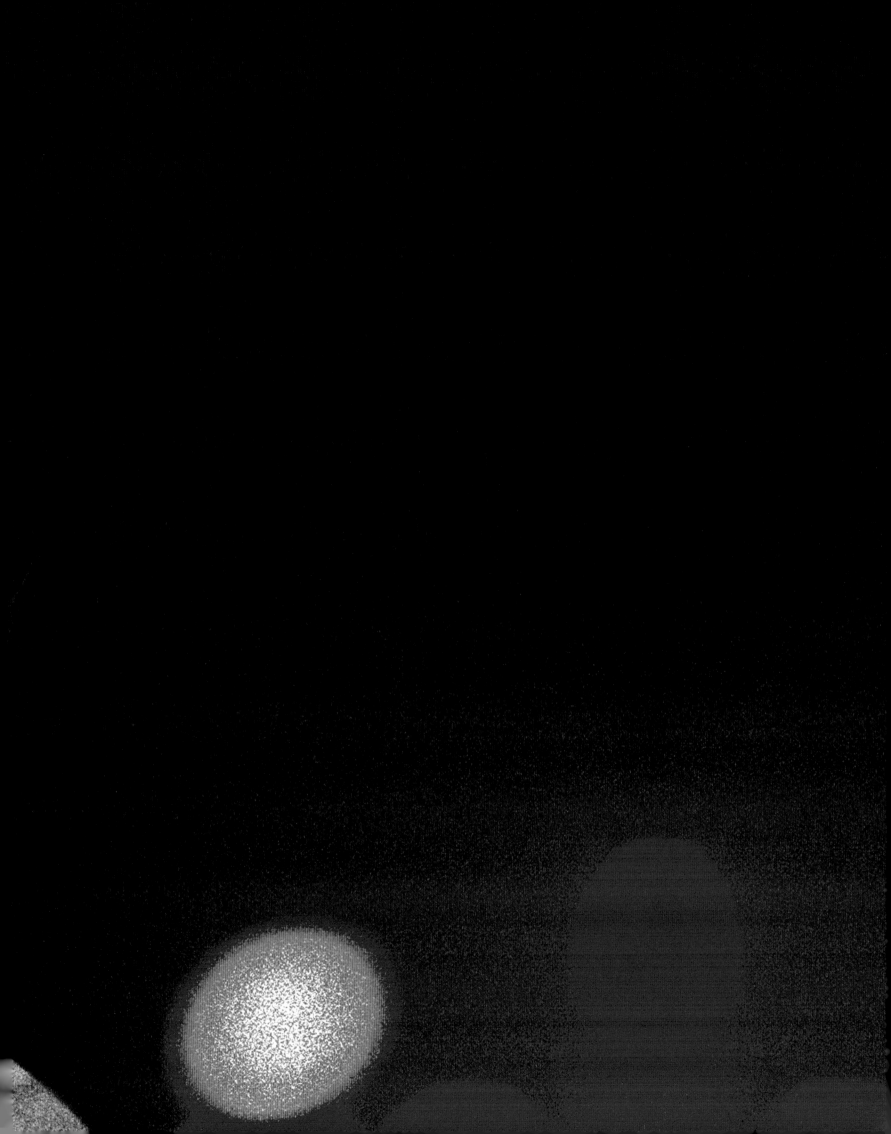

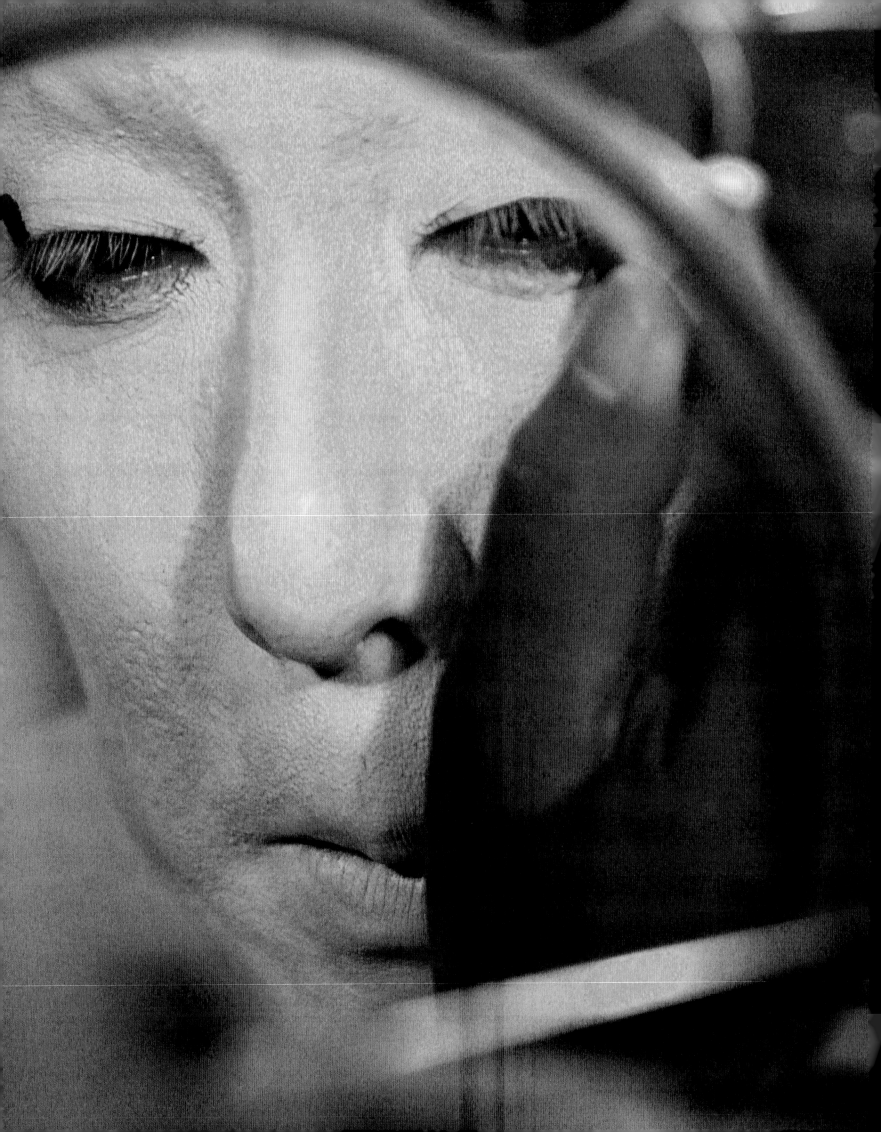

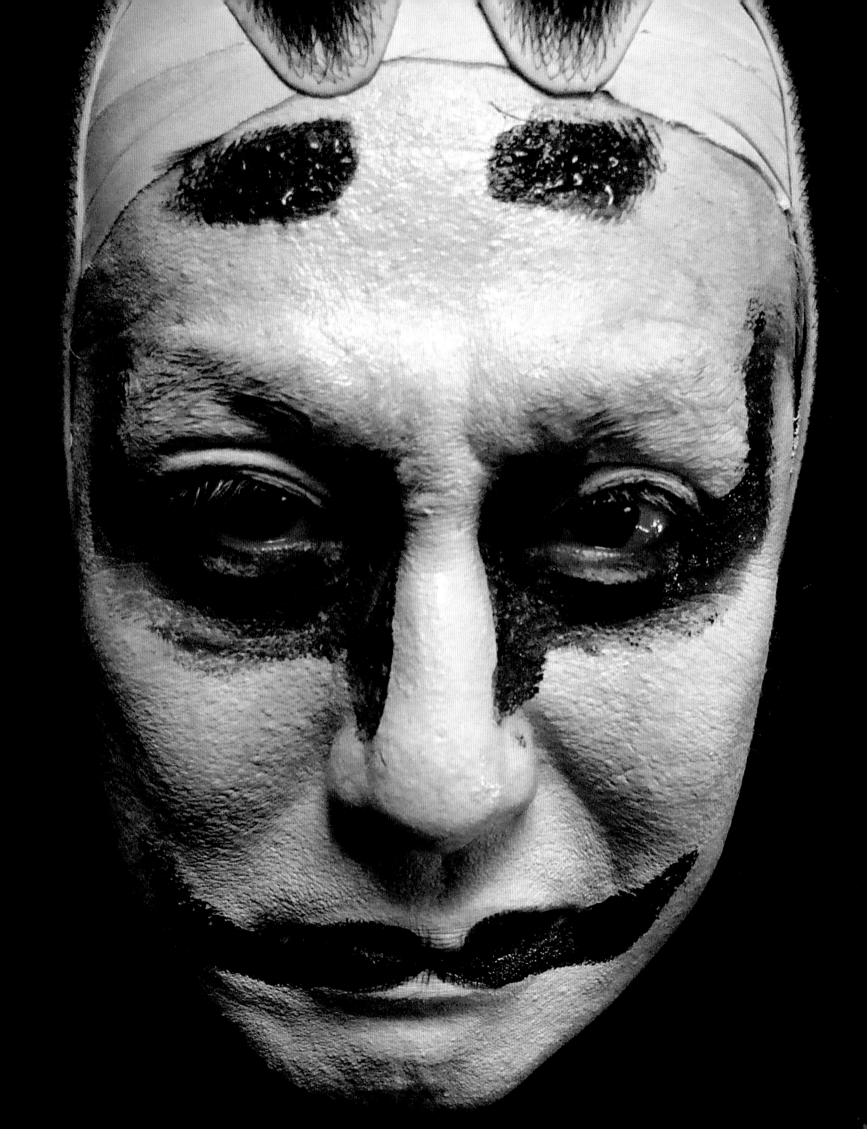

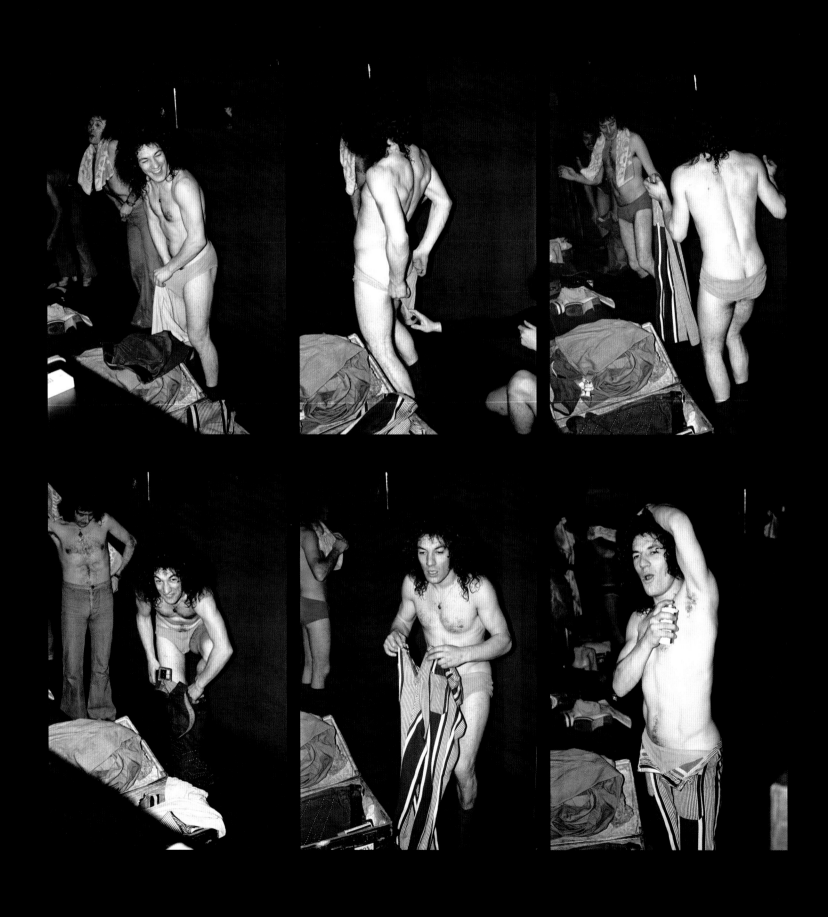

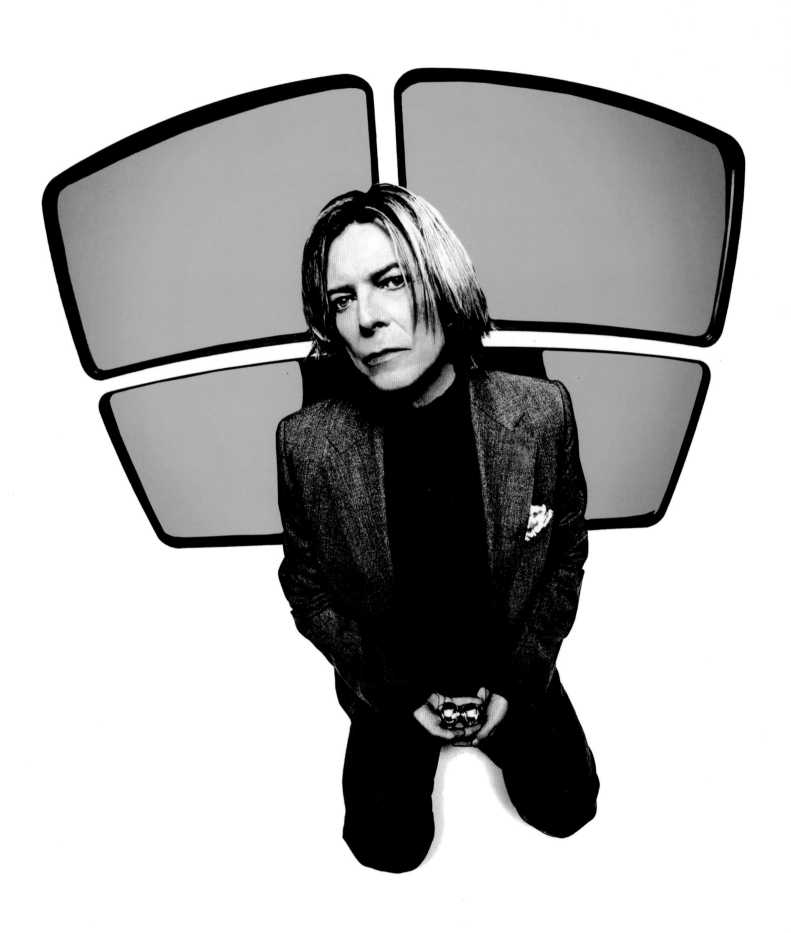

Medusa New York, 1982

Shot at my studio at Lexington Avenue and 32nd Street. I was planning a book called *Originals*, but the book never happened. It was too early in my career. I wanted a cover to express my "glam/punk" obsession, but also one that would make a statement about my relationship to the camera: "beguiled by film." The hair/film was by Wendy Kessel, a great hairstylist who I worked with occasionally.

Mick Rock 1969

I have no idea who took this shot. It popped up recently. It was buried away in some old box for decades. It's blurry, but that only seems to add a quality of having been taken long ago. I'm holding a light meter and wearing the round prescription spectacles like John Lennon used to favor at the time.

Syd Barrett London, 1969

Shot at Wetherby Mansions, Earls Court. Taken at Syd's flat with its unfinished painted floor and his record turntable. I've often been asked what the record was, but I can't remember, and the label isn't clear enough as it's burned out by the daylight coming through the window, which was the light source. The years have proven it to be probably the most iconic photo ever of Syd.

David Bowie, Iggy Pop, Lou Reed London, 1972

Shot at the Dorchester Hotel. "The Terrible Trio" or "The Unholy Trinity"—the only time these three have ever been photographed together. This isn't the famous version of this photo, with David and Iggy's manager Tony Defries grinning in the background, but this version has not been published before now.

Iggy & The Stooges London, 1972

Shot at Fulham Road Rehearsal Studios. They were rehearsing songs for the *Raw Power* album, with James Williamson on lead guitar and Ron Asheton on bass. It was a dark, dank basement, particularly appropriate for the still very much "underground" Stooges. Of that day, Iggy writes in the foreword to my photobook *Raw Power*: "Mick Rock was a breath of fresh air. . . . happily corruptible but not yet corrupted."

Freddie Mercury and **Brian May** London, 1974

Shot at the Rainbow Theatre, Finsbury Park. Note Freddie's teeth in all their magnificent overbite. He once told me he had four extra teeth in the back of his mouth but he would never have them removed because he believed they expanded his palette and that gave him his extraordinary vocal range.

The Agony & the Ecstasy UK, 1973

These were two very young Ziggy fans. As well as appealing to highbrow critics and intellectuals who were fascinated by his lyrical virtuosity and the intelligence manifested in the interviews he gave, Ziggy/Bowie had an enormous teen following. Many of them imitated Ziggy's golden circle on his forehead when they attended his concerts.

Dude 72 London, 1972

I was looking for a cover image for Mott the Hoople's Bowie-produced album *All the Young Dudes*, and photographed a slew of young boys in different circumstances around London. This, of course, would have been the perfect cover shot. I even got a photo release from the boy's parents. I've discussed with Ian Hunter in the years since how it slipped through the net, but still can't figure it out.

Tom Stoppard New York, 2008

Shot at the 60 Thompson Hotel. Tom tells of our first meeting in his very clever and charming foreword. A couple of months later he was in town to rehearse a new play, and took time out with me and my camera. When he saw the results he said they were the most flattering he'd seen of himself!

David Bowie London, 1973

Shot at an Oxford Street studio. A *Pin Ups* session outtake. He has occasionally played sax on records over the years, including tenor and alto saxes on *Pin Ups*. It's like a transitional picture: he still has the Ziggy hairdo but without all the glitzy makeup and clothes. I recall the suit was by Tommy Nutter.

David Bowie Beckenham, 1972

Shot at Bowie's home, Haddon Hall. I was contacted in 2001 by a gentleman who told me he'd acquired some original Bowie slides of mine, which he had come across in the archives of *Circus* magazine, and in return for a couple of signed Mick Rock prints he was happy to return them to me. I've saved first publication for the right occasion, and this is it! I'm glad to have it back!

Lou Reed London, 1972

Shot at King's Cross Cinema. The *Transformer* album cover. It was Lou's first ever concert in Europe. When I showed him the contact sheets, he was particularly keen to see a print of this shot. . . . I didn't notice the negative fall out of focus in the enlarger when I made the first test print, but the accident added another layer of mystery to the image. Lou knew immediately that this should be the cover for the album.

Lou Reed London, 1972

A *Transformer* session outtake. This slipped my eye over the years, and is published here for the first time. In his introduction to my first book Lou wrote: "Although Mick probably thought of himself as an outsider photographer, everyone else thought of him as another leg of the animal called 'rock': some even thought of him as a friend. . . . You can't buy Mick."

Lou Reed and **Nico** London, 1975

Shot at Blake's Hotel, South Kensington. Lou was playing the Hammersmith Odeon, and invited me to meet Nico. We had only met once before—I shot her with John Cale and Brian Eno for the *June 1, 1974* album cover. She said Lou was her younger brother in a former life. Of course, it's well known that they had an affair at the time of *The Velvet Underground* album with Andy Warhol's "banana" cover!

Lou Reed, Mick Jagger, David Bowie London, 1973

Shot at the Café Royale. This is often called "The Last Supper", being the afterparty for Ziggy Stardust's last-ever "live" performance, at Hammersmith Odeon. It was celebrity-stacked, with the likes of Bianca Jagger, Lulu, Ringo Starr, Jeff Beck, Keith Moon, Ryan O'Neal, and so on.

Iggy Pop London, 1972

Shot at Kings Cross Cinema. The Stooges first and only concert in the UK, until they reformed a few years ago: A concert now shrouded in mythology, though in fact it was only about 40 minutes long, but it was a revolution for all who were in attendance. Punk rock was never so raw and brutal.

Iggy Pop London, 1972

Shot at Kings Cross Cinema. The *Raw Power* cover. It was apparently shot the day after Lou Reed's *Transformer* cover, although for years I thought they were a week apart! I probably couldn't believe I'd gotten that lucky two days in a row: two iconic images that were forever to define their now-legendary subjects!! They're always a pair in my mind—both performance shots, but both quiet reflective moments.

Iggy Pop London, 1972

Shot at Kings Cross Cinema. This set includes the backbend shot, which is almost as iconic as the actual cover photo. I have a flood of great images from this one concert, probably my all-time favorite "live" shoot. Many years later I wrote: "Iggy was like something caged, and very angry about it. Something dreamed up by Karl Jung. That night I was a fascinated gamehunter with a loaded lens."

Rory Gallagher UK, 1972

Centrefold for his *Live in Europe* album. This was my third cover shoot for Rory. In 1971 I did an interview with him where he said: "In fifty years I'd like to be respected the way I dig any of the traveling guitar pickers like Leadbelly, Muddy Waters, Howlin' Wolf, Jack Elliott. . . ." He certainly achieved that. Eric Clapton once called him "the man who got me back into the blues."

Michael Stipe New York, 2005

Shot in an old warehouse on West 18th Street. Part of a *film noir* fashion layout for the French music and fashion publication *Rebel*. I was thinking of Bogart in his 1940s gumshoe roles or Fred MacMurray in *Double Indemnity*. Although unusual for him, I think Michael liked himself in the array of hats and suits the stylist conjured up for him.

Yeah Yeah Yeahs New York, 2003

Shot at 28th Street Studios. Outtake from *Vanity Fair* magazine session. This was around the time of their first CD release. This particular shot was later published in *Mojo* in July 2003 with an article extolling their virtues by yours truly, and has been in many of my gallery exhibitions.

Johnny Marr New York, 2003

Shot at Milk Studios, West 15th Street. Outtake from *Rebel* magazine session. The ex-guitarist for the Manchester band The Smiths, fronted by Morrissey, it was my first meeting with him, although I've shot him several times since. He told me that my old friend Mick Ronson was his biggest influence. Certainly he has Mick's amazing range and virtuosity. This is the first publication of this photo.

John Cale London, 1975

Taken at the time of the release of his album *Slow Dazzle*. I also have photos of the other members of his band that night, including Brian Eno, Chris Spedding, and the producer Chris Thomas. For me this picture echoes my *Transformer* photo of his fellow Velvet Underground founding member Lou Reed, but it's published here for the first time.

Cockney Rebel London, 1974

Shot at my Great Newport Street studio. Outtake from *The Psychomodo* album session. When Bowie discarded his "glam" skin in 1973, Rebel's Steve Harley was dubbed the main pretender to the "glam rock" crown. But he was no copyist, as his work bears witness, including their mega-hit single "Make Me Smile (Come Up and See Me)." I saw him play again recently and he's still a powerful performer.

Brian Eno, Nico, Kevin Ayers, John Cale London, 1974

Shot at the Rainbow Theatre, Finsbury Park. Outtake from the *June 1, 1974* cover session. The album was unique (besides the musicians, which also included Robert Wyatt and Mike Oldfield) because it was released just 27 days after the concert. It was the first time I had met Nico, who did a memorable rendition of The Doors' "The End."

Madonna New York, 1980

Shot at my Lexington Avenue studio. Bleecker Bob, owner of the famous Bleecker Bob's Golden Oldies record store in Greenwich Village, brought her to see me one evening. She was completely unknown at the time. I took some test snaps and thought no more about it, and even forgot I had them. It wasn't my idea for her to stick out her tongue—shows she was never the shy and retiring type!

Annabella Lwin Florida, 1982

Controversial teenage singer of Bow Wow Wow, managed by Malcolm McLaren. I went to Florida to shoot some photos of Joan Jett for a magazine, and shoot Bow Wow Wow for whom Joan's manager/producer Kenny Laguna was to produce their hit single "I Want Candy." I remember she told me she was already bored with the kind of publicity she had received. She felt she wasn't being taken seriously.

Kate Moss New York, 2002

Shot at Milk Studios West 15th Street. Outtake from *V* magazine session. This photo was a billboard in Las Vegas to promote an exhibition of mine in 2008. This was really an excuse for me and Kate to do a "glam/punk" session as a tribute to her idol Debbie Harry.

Kate Moss New York, 2002

The belt was given to me by Lou Reed. He had worn it at his *Rock n Roll Animal* concert. The pasties were by Agent Provocateur, hair by Gerald DeCock, styling by Avena Gallagher, makeup by Dick Page. Kate was the hostess for the launch party for my book *Picture This: Debbie Harry and Blondie* in 2004 when I was finally able to introduce them to each other.

Amanda Lear London, 1974

Shot at her flat in South Kensington. In the early 1970s she was known as a model—on the cover of Roxy Music's album *For Your Pleasure*— and as the band's muse, appearing with them on stage. In 1977 she took me to see Salvador Dali at the Plaza Hotel. He thought a "rock" photographer took photos of rocks! Of course he might have been putting me on. It was hard to tell.

Tina Turner London, 1974

Shot at the Odeon, Hammersmith. This was with the Ike & Tina Turner Revue who I saw at the same location again in 1975. On both occasions she wore terrific outfits that emphasized her legs and her animal/sexual energy, as in this photo. It was easy to understand Mick Jagger's claim that in the 1960s he had copied some of her moves.

Phil Lynott New York, 1977

Shot at the Photographics Unlimited Studios. I first met Phil in 1972 at the time of Lizzy's first hit single "Whiskey in the Jar" and we immediately bonded. He had everything—the talent, the looks, the charisma. With his hair-do he was like a tall Hendrix. Over the next few years I did several sessions of him with and without the band. Enough to fill a book, in fact.

Alex Kapranos New York, 2006

Shot in the East Village. The lead singer of Franz Ferdinand, this was an outtake from a session for an exhibition to celebrate Ray-Ban's 25th Anniversary of their Wayfarer sunglasses. A man with great natural looks, he was very easy to photograph. At the time of writing Franz Ferdinand haven't really broken out in America, but they're certainly one of the best of the UK's nouveau rock bands.

Tommy Lee Los Angeles, 2008

Outtake from *Mötley Crüe* session produced by Jennifer Ryan Jones for *Playboy*'s Men's Music Issue 2009. I hadn't photographed the band for 20 years. When Tommy saw this particular shot he emailed me: "Oh, Man . . . I farking love it!" So I sent him a signed print for his wall.

Lynyrd Skynyrd New York, 1998

Shot at the Eagle's Nest Studio. Billboard magazine's 25th anniversary tribute. This was one of two full-page photos, which their PR lady Laura Kaufman commissioned. Gary Rossington told me this was the best group photo ever taken of the band. He must have meant it because they insisted on doing a side deal for publicity usage.

Squeeze London, 1976

Shot at my Portland Road studio in Notting Hill Gate. Their manager Miles Copeland, who later managed The Police and Sting, told me he had a very young, unknown band (plus a modest budget) who had never been photographed before. They had no image and I wasn't sure what to do with them, so I did one setup that played off their name. I don't recall ever seeing this published.

Mick Ronson UK, 1973

My friend Mick, a sorely underappreciated talent as guitarist, arranger, and producer, who died far too soon, in 1993. Modestly stated, I consider this one of the finest live guitarist shots I've ever come across. This went astray until 1995 when I found it at a London syndication company I used to work with in the 1970s. It's amazing how lackadaisical I was in my early years in the game!

Richard Barone New York, 2007

Shot at the Gibson Entertainment Relations Rehearsal Studios, West 54th Street. Outtake from *Frontman: Surviving the Rock Star Myth* book cover session. Lead singer of The Bongos. On the back cover of the book I wrote " . . . he is a terrific photo subject and has so much 'front' that he was quite happy to pose naked in front of my lens for the cover of this book. Now that takes real 'front'!"

Alejandro Escovedo New York, 2008

Shot at Milk Studios, West 15th Street. An outtake from the cover session for his album *Real Animal*. This album was produced by longtime Bowie producer Tony Visconti. A critically acclaimed songwriter, he pointed out to me when I got to the session that I had photographed him in the late 1970s with his first group The Nuns from San Francisco, a punk rock band.

Pete Yorn Chicago, 2009

Shot at the W Hotel. Starwood Hotels and Sony Records promo session. I was aware of movies he has contributed music to, including *Spiderman* and *Shrek 2*, but I didn't realize what a cool performer he was until I saw him play later that day. I noted a big female following: "That's the upside of my music no doubt. It has a lot of appeal for the right sex!"

Daniel Merriweather Montreal, 2009

Shot at the W Hotel. Starwood Hotels and Sony Records promo session. Discovered by producer Mark Ronson and a star in his native Australia, Daniel's debut album *Love and War* hit UK #2 in 2009. Though relatively inexperienced he was fun to photograph, and he posted on his blog: "Mick Rock is one of the funniest geezers I've ever come across!"

Sondre Lerche New York, 2004

Shot at Drive In Studios. Outtake from *Two Way Monologue* album cover session. I was invited to see him perform at the Bowery Ballroom, assuming from the name that it was a French female singer—in fact he is probably Norway's top musical male export! We dined after the show, and planned for me to shoot his album cover when he returned to New York a few weeks later.

Wayne Kramer New York, 1983

Shot at my Lexington Avenue studio. I can't remember the purpose of the session. I knew of Kramer as lead guitar player of the MC5, Detroit's radical 1960s rock band, managed by John Sinclair, left-wing writer and founder of the White Panther Party. Wayne had also done two years in gaol for drug possession, which only added to his hip credibility. This great shot has barely seen the light of publication.

Rufus Wainwright New York, 2009

Shot at the Norwood Club. We met at the birthday afterparty for Bono's boyhood friend and singer Gavin Friday and decided it was about time we did a session. Although a showman with a great stage presence, I see his spirit as essentially that of a poet. That is reflected in the photo I chose for the book.

Bobby Gillespie London, 2006

Shot in a pub in London's East End. Outtake from Ray-Ban promotional/exhibition series. I've long been a fan of Bobby and the band, and have shot them on three occasions. But it was their album *Riot City Blues* that really captivated me, especially the single "Country Girl", which is a mainstay of my photographic and occasional DJ sessions.

Maxwell Los Angeles, 2009

Shot at Milk Studios. Outtake from *Playboy's* Music Issue 2010 session. Styled by Jennifer Ryan Jones with background by Eyal Baruch. I first met him a couple of years previously, and we discussed a session "when the time was appropriate." With his brilliant comeback album after seven years' silence, *Black Summer's Night*, with its six Grammy nominations for 2010, the time was obviously "appropriate."

Peter Gabriel London, 1973

Shot at my flat in King's Cross. I'd shot him a couple of weeks earlier with Genesis. "Dada" was the keyword for our approach, and he arrived with a bunch of eccentric paraphernalia. There's a shot of him with the stocking over his head and his right forefinger to his lips that's been on several magazine covers in recent years, but the shot here has never previously been let loose!

Jimmy Fallon New York, 2002

Shot at Milk Studios. Ex-*Saturday Night Live* alumnus and current late-night talk show host, Jimmy and I connected through his Syd Barrett obsession. Thus he invited me to take the cover and package photos for his Interscope musical parody album *Bathroom Wall*. I've photographed him several times since.

Phil Collins London, 1973

Shot in Steve Hackett's flat in Notting Hill. A Genesis group session for *Music Scene* magazine. At the time they were what later became known as an "alternative" band. They had a serious following, but had not yet broken commercially. Phil looks so young, with a full head of hair. The time has come to put this shot out for general consumption!

Waylon Jennings New York, 1972

Shot at RCA Recording Studios. RCA needed some publicity photos, and we only had an hour together. He talked about being Buddy Holly's bass player; he was scheduled to be on the ill-fated flight that killed Buddy in February 1959, but a last-minute decision kept him off it. He sang Buddy's "I'm Gonna Love You Too" during the session. This photo appeared on Waylon's 1973 album *Lonesome, On'ry and Mean*.

Ian Hunter New York, 1989

Shot at my studio on Mercer Street. An outtake from the cover shoot for the Hunter/Ronson Band album *Yui Orta*, the last of their many collaborations, mostly for Ian's solo albums. I have many photos of Ian, starting with Mott the Hoople at the time of *All the Young Dudes*. This is a different and unusual view which emphasizes his terrific jawline, published here for the first time.

Ray Davies New York, 1972

Shot in his hotel room. Ray was in town promoting the Kinks' album *Celluloid Heroes*, and RCA needed some promotional photos. I was traveling with minimal equipment and had no flash so I shot Ray close to the large windows, using the daylight which always gives a flattering look. Ray was in his full British mode and wore a cute light blue and purple pullover and a bowtie!

Cat Stevens (now Yusef Islam)
London, 1973

Shot in his manager Barry Krost's office, Mayfair. Outtake from the *Foreigner* cover session. Cat was introspective but polite, and the daylight through the window reflected his gentle mood. We later went to Hyde Park and took some more photos. He was happy with the pictures, which he thought appropriate for where he was at in that period of his transition.

Kelly Osbourne Los Angeles, 2002

Shot at Matchbox Studios. Kelly asked that I shoot the cover for her album *Shut Up!* She wanted the "punk/glam" aura of my Debbie Harry photos, which we used for reference while she was being made up. The results were "too sophisticated" for the record company, who wanted more of a "teen" look. Kelly was disappointed they didn't use them, so finally this shot can be seen!

Ozzy Osbourne London, 1974

Shot on the balcony of his manager's office in Mayfair. He was two hours late and apologized profusely. He explained that he was a very deep sleeper, and difficult to wake up. "That's why I couldn't hold down a regular job. I kept sleeping through the alarm in the morning. Thank God for rock 'n' roll!" Kelly told me this is her favorite session of her father: "He looks like a poet!"

Bryan Ferry London, 1974

Shot at the Royal Albert Hall. Roxy Music's original image was, like Bowie's Ziggy image, "spaceage glam." But when Bryan worked solo he adopted a classic "lounge lizard" look. For his first two appearances at London's prestigious venue he wore a full tuxedo and bow tie. In truth it suited his natural elegance. "I like to wear suits," he told me, "I feel comfortable in them."

Supergrass England, 2002

Shot at a photo studio in Brighton. Outtake from the *Life on Other Planets* session. EMI Records flew me into London from New York to shoot the band. With little sleep I was driven to Brighton, where a couple of the band members lived, the morning after my arrival. I shot many setups for several hours in three different places, and also found out why the band had chosen their name!

Wayne Coyne New York, 2006

Shot at Milk Studios. Outtake from *Playboy*'s Music Issue, March 2007 session. Wayne is lead singer with The Flaming Lips. The session was styled by Joseph DeAcetis. Wayne called me "sir" and "a master image maker." That guaranteed him some cool results! Bowie first turned me on to The Flaming Lips, and when I told Wayne he said he was "deeply flattered."

Pharrell Williams New York, 2008

Shot at Milk Studios. Outtake from *Playboy* session. A week after the shoot he provided my daughter Nathalie, a big fan, with two tickets to his concert with his band N.E.R.D in Miami, where she was at college. After the show he invited her and her friend backstage to do photos with him. A true gentleman. That scored me a lot of Daddy points with Nathalie!

Q-Tip New York, 2008

Shot at Milk Studios. Outtake from a *Playboy* session. Another shoot styled by Joseph DeAcetis. Q-tip loved the eyewear, although it wasn't present in the photo the magazine chose to publish. I called him Mr. Tip throughout the session, which he found amusing. "Why don't you just call me 'Q'?" he laughingly suggested.

Nas New York, 2008

Shot at the Milk Gallery. Outtake from "Nobody Was Thirsty" water charity promotional session. He was in a hurry because he was on a press run to promote his new album, simply called *Nas*, which had just gone to #1 in the US sales charts. "I'd like to stay longer," he said, "but my publicist won't let me!" Nevertheless everyone, including Nas, was happy with the results.

Chemical Brothers New York, 1999

Shot at Milk Studios. Outtake from *Surrender* album promo session. This was shot for their label Astralwerks. Errol Kolosine, the label head, warned me: "They're very boring to shoot. They don't really like photosessions." To jazz them up, I kept calling them the "Chemistry Sisters," which Errol tells me they still call themselves when they're in a self-deprecating mood.

The Prodigy New York, 2009

Shot at the 60 Thompson Hotel. Outtake from *Big Shot* magazine session. In an interview, Liam Howlett said: "Mick had so much energy. . . . At first I thought 'I'm not gonna get on with this guy' . . . but as soon as I started to speak to him, I really liked him. . . . It was a pleasure doing it . . . I hope we see him again." The pleasure was entirely mutual, I have to say.

The Killers New Orleans, 2005

Shot at a photo studio on the outskirts of the city. Styled by Joseph DeAcetis. This was my second session with the band, so they were used to me. I threatened to clean up my language, but they said they wouldn't shoot with me again if I did! There's a video of our first session on YouTube—a friend of my daughter told her that I used "every bad word in the known universe!"

Brandon Flowers New York, 2006

Shot at the Bar Niagara in the East Village. Outtake from Ray-Ban promo session. By now The Killers' Brandon had become a big international star, but, other than the bearded look and a more reflective attitude, it didn't seem to have affected him. The bar is co-owned by my friends, the singer Jesse Mallin and Johnny T.

The Big Pink New York, 2009

Shot at a loft in SoHo. Robbie Furze and Milo Cordell (son of the UK rock impresario Denny Cordell) invited me to listen to them at Electric Lady Studios. I was immediately impressed, so one afternoon thereafter I scaled the six flights of stairs to their loft and we got to work. One image from the session is included in their debut album package *A Brief History of Love*.

Joseph Arthur New York, 2008

Shot at the Milk Gallery. Outtake from "Nobody Was Thirsty" water charity promotional session. Not only a very talented musician and songwriter, Joe is also a very accomplished visual artist. When I sent this photo to him after the session, he emailed me back: "You definitely brought out the rent boy in me." So it's clear that Joe is a man of many talents!

Fotomaker New York, 1977

Shot at a studio on East 21st Street. The band consisted of Dino Danelli and Gene Cornish from The Rascals, Wally Bryson from The Raspberries, and Frankie Vinci. This eponymous first album wasn't successful, but the cover received a lot of attention. It gained a Grammy nomination, and press complaints about exploiting young girls. Both parents of Tiffany Power, the model, were at the session.

Golden Orb New York, 1983

Shot at my apartment on East 21st Street. CD cover for an obscure French rock act of the same name. They had little money but gave me carte blanche creatively, so I was happy to help. My "wild" reputation at the time had generally dampened enthusiasm for my skills, so I was happy to do the shoot. Plus I had a pretty model at hand, my then girlfriend (now wife) Pati!

David Bowie Aberdeen, 1973

Shot at the beginning of the final Ziggy Stardust tour. This has rarely been seen and is one of my favorite photos of David Bowie as Ziggy. What was he praying for? The continued rise of Ziggy Stardust, no doubt.

Richard Ashcroft Manchester, 2006

Shot at Old Trafford Cricket Ground. The biggest solo gig for the leader of The Verve, he was headlining a show that also included The Strokes and Razorlight. (The next day the Foo Fighters would headline). I was shooting for the event's sponsor, XFM Radio. I only had a few minutes before he went on, but I produced some memorable close-ups. This one is published for the first time.

Anton Newcombe Los Angeles, 1998

Outtake from the *Strung Out in Heaven* album session. Leader of The Brian Jonestown Massacre. My biggest problem was keeping certain members out of the toilet but I succeeded against all odds. Anton didn't particularly like this shot. I think he thought I was pulling his leg. But that's how I saw him: a "mad and bad angel"! Check out their eccentric antics in the documentary *Dig*!

Marianne Faithfull London, 1973

Shot at the Marquee Club. Outtake from *The 1980s Floor Show*. It was David Bowie's final performance as Ziggy Stardust in the US TV show, in which Marianne duetted with David on "I Got You Babe." She never looked so angelic!

Dolly Parton London, 1976

Shot at the Empire Pool, Wembley. Probably the biggest UK Country Music event to that date, it also featured Tammy Wynette and Loretta Lynn. Dolly garnered her biggest audience response for her rendition of "Jolene," which had been a big sleeper hit in the UK. As you can see from the photo this was well before the advent of the new, sleeker Dolly that appeared in the 1980s.

Joss Stone New York, 2003

Shot in Times Square. This was her first US appearance. I believe she was still only fifteen around the time of her first album release, *The Soul Sessions*. She was just very giggly, laughing the whole time, and I spoke with her mother who was present backstage as I shot. It was for a special charity event organized by Volvo. Toots and the Maytals also played that night.

Natasha Bedingfield New York, 2008

Shot at the W Hotel, Union Square. Outtake from *A Pocket Full of Sunshine* album session. There was also a concert in the evening to promote the album, which was very successful. I was asked to shoot her by the Starwood Hotels and Sony Music—one of a series of artists and events for a special touring exhibition.

Riley Keogh New York, 2008

Shot at Splashlight Studios. Outtake from *City* magazine cover session. Styled by Julie Ragolia, hair by Raymond McLaren, and makeup by Alexandra Kwiatkowski. She's the daughter of Lisa Marie Presley and granddaughter of Elvis Presley. I was fascinated by how her facial structure resembles her grandfather. She recently told me: "I look more like Elvis in that session than in any other photos of me."

Nathalie Rock New Jersey, 1994

Shot on the New Jersey shore. Another of my all-time favorite subjects, my beautiful daughter Nathalie. I make no apologies for including it. This photo has long haunted me and makes a perfect pairing with Riley—the Elvis dress was from the legendary rock 'n' roll clothing store Trash and Vaudeville, at St. Mark's Place in New York's East Village.

Debbie Harry New York, 1978

Shot at East 21st Street. Outtake from *Viva* magazine feature session. My first session with the divine Ms. Harry, the greatest gift for photographers ever to emerge from the rock music world! The magazine ceased publication before the photo was published. However, it finally surfaced on a 1980 *Penthouse*—Debbie was tickled to be on the cover of a men's magazine, clothed in black up to her neck!

Debbie Harry New York, 1978

Shot at East 21st Street. She was never more the "Marilyn Monroe of Rock" than on that day. This particular frame only surfaced a couple of years ago from an ex-lady-friend's files, and has not been published before. The terrific hair and makeup was by my favorite of those years, Sharon Slattery.

Debbie Harry New York, 1978

Shot at East 21st Street. Top left image is a first-time publication, bottom left is arguably the most famous photo of Debbie. She once wrote: "My immediate impression of Mick was that he was very tall, very handsome, and quite mad. It seemed as if he was using sleight of hand in our sessions. I thought if Mick were to be a drag queen, his name would have been 'Miss Direction'!"

Debbie Harry New York, 1979

Shot at my studio on Lexington Avenue at 32nd Street. Her hair had been cut short by this time—she claimed she needed to do it because she'd overdyed it! The radios were gathered from a junk store on Canal Street, and I smashed them up even more. I think I was trying to make some kind of statement about punk, commerciality, and music!

Debbie Harry and **Karen O**
New York, 2006

Shot at Milk Studios. Outtake from *Dazed and Confused* magazine session. The magazine wanted "downtown divas, then and now." And they got New York's two most hip downtown girls of all time: The Original Punk Diva and The Nouveau Punk Diva, together in one frame. I was very spoiled that day!

Karen O New York, 2006

Shot at Milk Studios. Debbie had an appointment and had to leave after I had shot them together. But Karen elected to stay and play some more. And play we did. I have a bunch of wildly over-the-top images of her in various attires and attitudes. This shot is published here for the first time.

Pinkeye New York, 1984

Shot at my studio on Lexington Avenue at 32nd Street. An album cover for a Japanese band of the same name, I think the album title was *Look at This!* They were recording in New York and I met them through a mutual Japanese lady friend. The model was my girlfriend Pati again! She was conveniently cheap for certain low cost budgets of the time—and very tolerant of my particular brand of lunacy. . . .

Strapps London, 1976

Shot at my studio in Portland Road, Notting Hill. Fronted by the Aussie Ross Stagg, they wanted an S&M theme for their first album cover. It was walking the line, so we needed an image the record label wouldn't be afraid of using, but it was still subversive. It did stir up a few press comments, which everyone was happy to get. I did a group portrait for their second release the following year.

Carly Simon New York, 1980

Shot in the spring, at my studio on Lexington Avenue at 32nd Street. Outtake from *Come Upstairs* album session. I uncovered Carly's wild streak—I got her to roll on the floor, rip up the backdrop and chew on it. In another setup I had her spitting champagne at the camera! The record label found these too strong for her image, and picked a much "safer" photo from the session.

Kate Moss New York, 2002

Shot at Milk Studios. After the shot for *V* magazine we carried on. I shot over five hundred frames that day, all on film on my Hasselblad—I hadn't yet got into digital. I used 40mm and 50mm lenses to "punk" the photos out. I wanted "anti-fashion," a fusion of glam and punk. In 2009 I did exhibitions in Holland based around the Kate photos.

Sharon Foo New York, 2006

Shot at Milk Studios. Outtake from *Playboy*'s 2007 Music Issue fashion session. From the Danish duo The Raveonettes, this was styled by Joseph DeAcetis. Classically beautiful with her facial bone structure, she reminds me of a tall Debbie Harry in her younger days. But I sensed she didn't want to overplay her physical charms. This shot however caught what I saw in her and was determined to capture.

Lady Gaga New York, 2008

Shot at Splashlight Studios. Outtake from *City* magazine session. Styled by Julie Ragolia, hair by Raymond McLaren, and makeup by Alexandra Kwiatkowski. At the time of the shoot she was still completely unknown. Late in the session she confidently announced to me: "I'm gonna be a huge star within the next few months." She turned out to be more than accurate in her prognostication!

Jack White London, 2006

Shot in Hyde Park. One of the sponsors was XFM, and I was shooting anything and everything that popped up, including Jack, whom I shot with various people, including Kate Moss and members of The Strokes. He was headlining with his great band The Raconteurs, and he even invited me onstage during the performance to photograph, which I knew was a mark of respect since he's such a private person.

Ziggy Marley New York, 2009

Shot at The Gates private club on 8th Avenue. It was a birthday party for an executive of Spike TV, with an unannounced appearance by Ziggy Marley, apparently a friend of several of the Spike people. He channeled his extraordinary father when he performed several of his songs, including the hymnal "Redemption Song." Later I hung out with him and talked of meeting Bob, and took a series of photographs.

Bob Marley London, 1975

Shot at the Odeon, Hammersmith. He played two nights, and I was in the pit with my camera for both. It was the closest I'd come to a religious experience at a concert. At the afterparty, where I briefly partook of a puff with a broadly grinning Bob, I told him how I'd felt, and he replied "Ah, man, but the religious experience is more fun than anything in life!"

Jimmy Cliff London, 1972

Shot outside the Island Records building in Notting Hill. It was a session for the label around the time of the release of *The Harder They Come*, the classic reggae film which starred Jimmy. He didn't have a lot to say but was very easy to shoot. This frame makes its publishing debut here.

Wilson Pickett New York, 1999

Shot at Studio 900. Back cover for *It's Harder Now* album. I also shot the front cover but I prefer this one. It was his last album, he died in 2006, and I often play it on my photosessions. The director D. A. Pennebaker was filming a documentary that day about aging soul singers called *Only the Strong Survive*, in which there's a clip of me lensing Wilson.

Snow Patrol New Orleans, 2004

Outtake from *Playboy*'s Music Issue, March 2005 session. Styled by Joseph DeAcetis. They were a new name, but I liked the single "Chocolate" from their album *Final Straw*. I played it throughout the session, much to their amusement. They said their melodic romantic music was very popular with the ladies. Gary Lightbody, the lead singer and songwriter, told me "our audiences are 75–80% female."

Queens of the Stone Age
Los Angeles, 2007

Shot in a rundown motel. Outtake from *Era Vulgaris* album session. Josh Homme invited me to do the session. For one of the setups he wanted ventriloquist dummies, so the day before we trolled around a huge prop warehouse in search of suitable china partners, featured here. There's something comedic, and a little perverse, in their flirtation with the dummies.

Perry Farrell Los Angeles, 2007

Shot at Playboy Studios. I have photographed Perry (of Jane's Addiction fame) several times in recent years, and he's a very sensitive and cooperative subject. This may not be the most flattering image I've ever snapped of him, but I love the tentacle-like effect of the hands. It makes for a very memorable image. I know he agrees!

David Bowie London, 1976

Shot at Wembley Empire Pool. This was in David's "Thin White Duke" era, a tour to promote his *Station to Station* album. His only UK dates were six nights at the Empire Pool. He did have an interesting look at that moment in time. I'm sure this shot was taken while he sang the lyrics ". . . my brain hurts a lot" from the superb song "Five Years."

David Bowie and **Mick Ronson**
UK, 1973

Shot in a British Rail dining car, between London and Aberdeen. I traveled up and down the UK during the final Ziggy tour, but until my book *Moonage Daydream*, this photo was never published. It's now one of the most popular images in my exhibitions—something to do with the mundanity of the meal and the ridiculously exotic look of the diners!

Bryan Ferry London, 1975

Shot at his house in Holland Park Avenue. I did several sessions with Bryan and Roxy Music in the early and mid-70s. At the time of this shoot he was enjoying a big international hit with the single release from *Siren*, "Love Is the Drug." In a number of setups he wore this crumpled khaki suit which worked perfectly with his stylish, but relaxed, image. In truth Bryan could always wear any kind of suit and look cool.

Michael Bublé New York, 2009

Shot at Milk Studios. Outtake from *Playboy's* Music Issue, March 2010 session. Styled by Jennifer Ryan Jones. Michael showed up in casual attire, although his image is very suited, Sinatra-style. He admitted "Suits are my stage uniform." He was very gracious, and signed two CD covers—one for my mother, a huge fan, and one for my niece Lucinda, another enthusiast.

Thin Lizzy London, 1973

Shot at my apartment in King's Cross. Phil Lynott had a great self-deprecating sense of humor. He used to like to call himself a "lepracoon"—he was an Irishman, with a white mother and black father, who grew up in Dublin. This shot, which was published only once before, reflected the traditional Irish mystical side of his nature.

Thin Lizzy London, 1975

Shot at London Wharf. Outtake from *Jailbreak* album back cover session. I did this session, in a still broken-down area of London, for their upcoming album and for publicity. Phil was by then in love with the image of the band as a street fighting gang, thus the chains and knives. This is the first-time publication of this shot. I later shot the back sleeve for their 1977 album, *Bad Reputation*.

Hall & Oates New York, 1980

Shot at my Lexington Avenue studio. I was commissioned by Darryl and John's record company RCA to shoot promo shots for their *Voices* album, one of which would be the cover of *Cashbox* magazine. They wanted a tougher image, so I encouraged them to paint-spray the backdrop with the album title and rip it up.

Mötley Crüe Los Angeles, 1985

Outtake from *Theatre of Pain* album session. They were in the middle of their glam-metal mid-80s success and flew me to L.A to shoot promo photos for their third album. I did elaborate setups using broken mirrors, candles, and motorbike parts, and spent a lot of money by the standards of the time. The photos in the bubble bath were much in demand on the release of their autobiography *The Dirt*.

Michael Monroe New York, 1987

Shot on Avenue B, Lower East Side. Ex-singer with Finnish glam-metal band Hanoi Rocks, who were almost a prototype for Mötley Crüe. After a studio session with his new band Secret Chiefs, I went to Avenue B where he knew a derelict area with great graffiti. "I'm the 'Dream Angel from Space,'" he laughed, and like a cross between Marilyn Monroe and Mick Jagger, somehow he made complete sense!

Iggy Pop New York, 1981

Shot at my studio on 32nd and Lexington. Outtake from *Party* album session. For one setup I asked him to paint a Dali-esque clock on the white wall of the studio. I'd been checking out a book of Dali paintings, and had in mind his work *The Persistence of Memory*, with its "melting" clock faces. I showed it to Iggy, and he came up with his own punk/graffiti version.

Queen London, 1974

Shot at my first studio in Great Newport Street. Outtake from *Queen II* album cover session. The photo was copied 18 months later for their promo film for *Bohemian Rhapsody*. I had found a photo of Marlene Dietrich, showed it to Freddie, and it got him excited. The other three were a little hesitant, feeling it made them look pretentious. But they later agreed, as Freddie did a little arm twisting.

Queen London, 1974

Shot at my first studio in Great Newport Street. Outtake from *Queen II* album session. I took a lot of photos of this setup, mostly variations of the finger position of Freddie's hands, but, just to cover all the possibilities, I also tried switching John and Roger to different sides. I shot everything in both black and white and color. This is a good occasion to flush some of the variations out of the closet!

Freddie Mercury London, 1974

Shot at my first studio in Great Newport Street. In the summer of 1974 I did several solo sessions with Freddie, and produced many great images. I came to regard him as a friend and he trusted my instincts about his image in that early period. This was one of his favorite portraits.

The Pointer Sisters London, 1974

Shot backstage at the London Palladium. Outtake from *Sunday Observer* magazine session. This was their first performance in the UK, and I occasionally shot for this magazine in those days. What I most remember is having to wait a couple of hours for Pierre LaRoche to do the makeup, which left me about ten minutes to grab the photos in the cramped space of the dressing room! I made the most of my time. . . .

Steve Van Zandt New York, 2005

Shot at Renegade Nation Studios, West 35th Street. Long-time Bruce Springsteen guitarist, in recent years he has produced a regular series of rock radio programs under the banner *Little Steven's Underground Garage*. I did a shoot for *Uncut* magazine, but took time to do some additional shots, including here in his personnal office, which certainly reflects the unconventional and dynamic force that he is!

Peter Gabriel UK, 1973

Shot at a live festival. Peter was then lead singer of Genesis. I can't remember what the exact occasion was, but he was in high theatrical mode. I have photos from that date of him in several different outfits. He was more theatrical in many ways than Bowie, but less "glam" and more "Dada." Certainly stranger!

Mick Jagger London, 1975

Shot at Earls Court Arena. The Stones biggest UK concert for their 1975–76 world tour, promoting their first album with Ronnie Wood, *Black and Blue*. A great piece of rock theater that featured the infamous giant inflatable penis for one number. This is a very popular print at my gallery exhibitions, maybe because it's got the lips and the flying hair that gives him that "rooster" look.

Iggy Pop New York, 1977

Shot at the Palladium (a.k.a. The Academy of Music), East 14th Street. The major New York show of Iggy's world tour to promote the Bowie-produced album *The Idiot*, with David himself on keyboards, and the Sales brothers, Hunt and Tony, as the rhythm section. It's one of my favorite live photos, and was featured in a compilation album package of Iggy's work.

Steve Tyler New York, 1976

Shot at Madison Square Garden. I had gotten to know Aerosmith's publicist, Laura Kaufman, and she secured a photopass for me to shoot the band, who at the time were regarded in my home country as a lighter-weight version of The Rolling Stones. After I saw their performance that night I completely revised my view of them. They were a rock 'n' roll band who delivered their own unique brand of magic.

Jerry Garcia London, 1972

Shot at the Empire Pool, Wembley. The first date of the first Grateful Dead tour outside of North America. I was late for the show, but I knew one of the promoters who snuck me in through the artists' entrance and got me a great view. I shot several very cool close-ups of Jerry, including this one where he looks like he's having a very good time.

Lou Reed US, 1976

Shot on the Rock and Roll Heart *album tour.* Lou flew me in to shoot and art direct the cover for his new album, and also to work with him on the video images which would be featured on a set of 60 TVs as the background to his touring stage set. I worked on the control board which fed the screens, and also doubled up as the tour photographer. In those days Lou still often smoked while he performed.

Daft Punk Las Vegas, 2007

They were headlining the Vegoose Festival. Iggy & The Stooges were also on the bill. I hung with the duo in the photostudio before the session. They were somewhat shy, skinny, and very polite. I spoke to them part of the time in French, their native language, which amused them, but they would not allow me to take any photos of them except in their techno/space outfits.

Peaches London, 2006

Shot at a small club in Mayfair. Outtake from Ray-Ban promotional session. This was taken at the time of her album *Impeach My Bush*. I'd seen her perform her racy act in New York, and wasn't sure what to expect. Fun to photograph, she assured me that (unlike her raunchy stage persona) she was a well-brought-up middle-class girl called Merrill Beth Nisker (in itself a pretty cool name).

Tania Maria New York, 1988

Shot at my SoHo studio, Mercer Street. Outtake from *Forbidden Colors* album session. Tania is a Brazilian singer/composer, mostly labeled as "jazz," although she covers a much broader range. The photo used by Capitol for the cover has the same background and scarf but reveals her face, but this is a favorite of mine for its aesthetic resonance, shown here for the first time.

Shemekia Copeland New York, 1997

I shot the cover for the debut album of 18-year-old Shemekia, *Turn the Heat Up*, on the Alligator Blues label. One of many children of blues legend Johnny Copeland, she was inexperienced but a sweet young lady, with a voice that sounded like a much older person. We got some superb photos, although they used one of the test Polaroids. The photo debuting here is the one I lobbied for.

Tori Amos New York, 1996

Outtake from *Musician* magazine session. Shot just after the release of her album *Boys for Pele*. Makeup was by Kevyn Aucoin, who'd worked for *Vogue* and other celebrities, and died in 2002. Somehow Tori reminded me of a red-haired Debbie Harry. I remember that I had my blue *Penthouse* cover in mind as I shot, certainly I applied the same high lighting.

Bebe Buell New York, 1980

Shot at my studio on Lexington Avenue. I first met Bebe in 1977, pregnant with her daughter Liv Tyler and living with Todd Rundgren. I can't remember what this session was for, probably we just wanted to do it, but I remember her then boyfriend, Stiv Bators of The Dead Boys, was present. This shot is published for the first time. In 2001 I shot the cover for her biography *Rebel Heart*.

Alicia Keys London, 2009

Shot at Aqua club/restaurant, Regent Street at the Element of Freedom *album launch.* The launch was sponsored by Sony Music and Starwood Hotels. I was to have 35 minutes before she did the red carpet walk, but everything ran late and I ended up with just 15 minutes backstage. I kissed her hand, told her it was a privilege to shoot her, and she gave me wonderful images!

Patti Labelle London, 1975

A London theater performance of Labelle at the time of their hit "Lady Marmalade." Their costumes were designed by Larry Legaspi who described his style as "Space Deco"—he designed the band Kiss' stage costumes. It gave Labelle a "glam rock" look, unique in a black act. I hung out with manager Vicki Wickham and the girls after the show. They were fascinated that most of the audience were young and white.

Joan Jett New York, 1981

Shot at my studio on 32nd and Lexington Avenue. The *I Love Rock 'n' Roll* album cover. They'd already had two unsuccessful sessions before I was approached, and had very little money left. Of course I agreed, and out of it came her most famous photo. I thought of her as a "female Elvis" when I shot this particular setup. In 2008 I shot her again for the first time in many years. She's still a beautiful subject.

Siouxsie Sioux New York, 1980

Shot at my studio on Lexington Avenue. She was the UK's primary female punk rocker, and I was intrigued. I shot a bunch of frames with her and the band, but spent the majority of the session focused on Siouxsie. Very easy to photograph, she was a natural ham with great presence. One of the photos from this setup ended up on the cover of a US single release.

Asia Argento California, 2003

Shot at Danielle Steele's summer house in Napa Valley. Romantic novelist Danielle's son set it up, orginally for the *New York Times* color supplement. It also involved the JT LeRoy family and the rock band Third Eye Blind. For some complicated political reasons the feature never ran, but I took some memorable images including a lot of Asia, the controversial Italian film actress and director.

Juliette Lewis New York, 2007

Shot in the dressing room at the Beacon Theater. I'd seen Juliette in the UK a year earlier with her band The Licks, and was impressed with her wild and uninhibited performance, so when her PR offered to set up a session I was very enthusiastic. I went to the Beacon the afternoon of her performance, and her zaniness clicked with me instantly. It's the first publication of this image.

Hedwig and the Angry Inch
New York, 2001

Shot at Milk Studios. A stage musical that had acquired a cult following in New York, I'd gotten to know the writer/director/lead actor John Cameron Mitchell. So when he asked me to shoot the poster and promo photos for a film version, I was flattered and delighted. It's the closest thing to *The Rocky Horror Picture Show* which I'd shot some 27 years previously.

JT LeRoy New York, 2002

Shot at the Chelsea Hotel. I had totally bought into the myth of JT LeRoy, the literary identity hoax. The true writer of the cult books is Laura Albert, but the person who played the role of the boy "JT" turned out to be a girl, Savannah Knoop. The convoluted tale behind the hoax only makes me love this image even more! If you don't know about it, check it out!

GhostLipps New York, 1986

Shot at my studio on Mercer Street, SoHo. It was the cover and title for a single release for a briefly formed German band called MeisterZen. It was only released in Germany. It was a small budget, but gave me another opportunity to produce an image without a brief, and do exactly my own interpretation. This is a chance to display it to a much wider audience.

Wild Angel London, 1976

Shot at my studio in Notting Hill Gate. Outtake from *Wild Angel* album session. Lou Reed produced an album for Nelson Slater, but Nelson didn't want to be on the cover, and the title was *Wild Angel.* It turned out that the cover was far wilder than the music and it caught some flak in *Newsweek* and other magazines in features about the exploitation of women in rock 'n' roll and fashion photography.

Johnny Winter New York, 1988

Shot at my studio on Mercer Street, SoHo. I had photographed Johnny in London in the 1970s, including the performance photo for his 1976 album *Captured Live!* The art director Ioannis knew he wanted a closeup of Johnny's tattoo for the front cover, after that I could shoot what I wanted. I produced two to three hundred memorable pix of him that day, including this one, published for the first time.

Smutty Smiff New York, 1999

Shot at a friend's studio. I had known Smutty for 20 years, since he showed up in New York as bass player with the UK rockabilly band The Rockats and became a favorite subject of hip fashion photographers. For this session he was in town to find photos for a book on tattoos he was doing. He gave me some memorable images, including this one, which now surfaces for the first time.

Michael Clark London, 2009

Shot at the Columbia Hotel, Lancaster Gate. The dancer-choreographer was working on a production based on the music of Bowie, Lou Reed, and Iggy Pop, and wanted to license my *Unholy Trinity* photo for promotion. A subsequent exciting session produced a slew of great photos, including this one. He reminded me a lot of my old friend Lindsay Kemp, but more punk, less Cocteau.

Lindsay Kemp London, 1974

Shot at my studio in Great Newport Street. Outtake from *Observer* magazine session. The great British mime/choreographer mentored David Bowie in the art of mime, makeup, and costume in the late 1960s. I shot Lindsay many times over the years, and have on occasion been approached about doing a book on him. In the meantime he's often graced my exhibitions—this shot in particular.

Queen London, 1974

Shot at my studio in Great Newport Street. Outtake from *Queen II* album cover session. It was Freddie's mirror, and since he'd taken the trouble to bring it along and squeeze it into the tiny elevator without damaging it, I was happy to shoot a variation on the main setup. I'm very glad I did. This photo is in the permanent collection of the National Portrait Gallery in London.

David Bowie Beckenham, 1972

Shot at Bowie's home, Haddon Hall. Reviewing this session, David told his manager "Mick sees me the way I see myself." It was the moment that sealed our working relationship, two months before the release of the Ziggy Stardust album. After that all bets were off! The first two publications of this photo were in men's magazines in 1972: the first in *Club International* in the UK, then American *Playboy*.

Kanzaburo Nakamura Tokyo, 2005

Shot at Kabuki-za Theatre. After the launch of my retrospective in Tokyo in 2003, the producers asked me what I would like to do next in Japan. "Shoot Kabuki theatre," was my immediate response. So they contacted the agents of Kanzaburo, Japan's foremost Kabuki director/actor, who was setting up a production at New York's Lincoln Center in the summer of 2004.

Kanzaburo Nakamura New York, 2004

Shot at the Lincoln Center. They allowed me full run over four days: backstage, dressing rooms, set preparations, rehearsals, performances, they even let me do a makeshift setup for portraits. In 2005 they flew me to Tokyo and gave me the same access over several days, unprecedented for a non-Japanese photographer. Overall I shot some 5000 photos in Tokyo alone.

Kanzaburo Nakamura New York, 2004

Shot at the Lincoln Center. In April 2007 they again flew me to Tokyo to launch two book collaborations with Kanzaburo, one a limited edition boxed version, the other a commercial version, and an impressive 120 print exhibition of my *Kabuki* photos at the Tokyo Midtown Gallery. Both books and the exhibition were titled *Tamashii: Mick Rock Meets Kanzaburo*. *Tamashii* means "soul" in Japanese.

Kanzaburo Nakamura Tokyo, 2005

Shot at Kabuki-za Theatre. In his introduction to the books, Kanzaburo says: "As I look at these pictures I realize that Mick takes photographs with his heart. He captures the essence of his subjects no matter where they come from. . . . We are the same at the bottom of our souls. . . . so I was really in tune with Mick. We made a profound connection. He is a total master of his art. He is my friend."

Tim Curry Bray, Berkshire, 1974

Shot on the set at Bray Film Studios. Outtake from *The Rocky Horror Picture Show*. Director Jim Sharman invited me to take photos of the filming. Other than the continuity photographer, no other photographer was allowed on the set. I took many portraits of Tim as Frank-N-Furter, including this one of him in his laboratory tunic and rubber gloves, which he wore when he brings his "creation" to life.

Richard O'Brien Bray, Berkshire, 1974

Shot on the set at Bray Film Studios. Outtake from *The Rocky Horror Picture Show*. He was the author and composer of the film and also plays Riff Raff in the movie. In his foreword to my photo homage to the production *Rocky Horror*, Richard writes: "How glad I am that director Jim Sharman felt moved to invite Mick down to Bray Studios during filming and how glad I am that he accepted."

Susan Sarandon Bray, Berkshire, 1974

Shot on the set at Bray Film Studios. Outtake from *The Rocky Horror Picture Show*. Susan Sarandon plays Janet in the movie and at the time she was a young and barely known actress, but perfectly cast for the role. She certainly cuts a desirable figure when she is transformed from her attitude of sexual innocence to the scenes where she sports the corset and garter belt.

Meat Loaf Bray, Berkshire 1974

Shot on the set at Bray Film Studios. Outtake from *The Rocky Horror Picture Show*. Meat Loaf was Eddie in the movie. He was unknown at the time and happy to mug for my stills camera while awaiting his turn in front of the movie camera. I next met him a few years later in Woodstock where he was working with producer Todd Rundgren on his debut album *Bat out of Hell*, which propelled him to international fame.

The Scissor Sisters New York, 2007

Shot at Industria Photo Studio. Outtake from *Ta-Dah* album session. The band invited me to do the session and, as a fan of their live shows, I was delighted. At one point they emailed me that I was their favorite rock photographer! Among the top nouveau rock acts, although more popular in the UK and Europe than in the United States.

Jake Shears New York, 2007

Shot at Industria Photo Studio. One of the great modern frontmen, The Scissors Sisters' Jake was happy to cooperate when I suggested we do an extended solo workout. At times he reminds me of Ziggy/Bowie, as this particular image bears witness. He's a natural in front of the camera.

Har Mar Superstar New York, 2009

Shot at the Ace Hotel. Outtake from *Dark Touches* album session. I first met Sean Tillman (his given name) in 2004 when he performed at a party to launch my Debbie Harry and Blondie book. An uninhibited performer and a great songwriter, he was in New York for the release of his latest album and we decided it was time for us to do a session to help promote it. I wanted him to look like Geronimo.

Todd Rundgren Woodstock, 1977

Todd needed some promotional photos for his third album with his band Utopia, so invited me to Woodstock, where he was producing Meat Loaf's first album *Bat out of Hell*. He was also rehearsing for a Utopia tour. I shot the group around the backdrop for their live show, including this enormous Egyptian-style gold mask. I couldn't resist the temptation to lens Todd peering though one of the eyes.

Zak Starkey New York, 2006

Shot at Madison Square Garden. He needed photos for *Drum* magazine, and for an ad for drumsticks he was endorsing. He was in New York for two nights with The Who. I shot the photos during The Who's soundcheck. He told me that Pete Townsend had told him he was "the drummer whose style most closely resembled that of original Who drummer Keith Moon." A compliment indeed for Ringo's son!

Eugene Hütz Las Vegas, 2007

Outtake from *Playboy's* Music Fashion Issue 2008 session. Styled by Jennifer Ryan Jones. Born in the Ukraine, he is lead singer with Gogol Bordello, the gypsy punk band who'd just released their fourth album *Super Taranta!* He was a very animated subject and clearly loved the camera, and I snapped a slew of great pix. In 2008 he was lead character in Madonna's directorial film debut *Filth and Wisdom*.

Snoop Dogg California, 2009

Shot at the Portraits By Kathy photo studio, Covina. This was produced by Jen Ryan Jones, with backgrounds by Eyal Baruch. It was an hour's drive outside L.A, where Snoop was coaching his son's schoolboy football team. Shooting in this local studio, we talked for hours, and started discussing our backgrounds—and he told me he was half Italian! It explains his uncharacteristically sharp features.

Lou Reed London, 1975

Shot at my studio in Great Newport St. Album cover for *Coney Island Baby.* Often in the early to mid-70s, Lou would come to London and we'd take photos that would appear on album covers or in the press. I was also the art director on this one, and received a Grammy nomination for album cover of the year, plus several other awards.

Lou Reed London, 1975

Shot the same day, Lou has often described this session as his favorite of all. He'd just bought a bunch of clothes from a shop called Ian's on St. Marks Place in New York's East Village, and wanted to parade them in front of my lens. We produced many images that day which would later qualify as "classics." Some images have appeared on covers of compilation albums.

Can London, 1975

Shot at my studio in Portland Road, Notting Hill Gate. Outtake from *Landed* album session. This was at the time the influential Krautrock luminaries Can released their album *Landed*. Their record label Virgin decided they needed some promo photos, and the band wanted to work with me. I also saw and photographed them playing a couple of nights later.

Brian Johnston London, 1973

I can't remember where these were shot, but it was backstage after a gig. Brian was getting changed after an impressive performance. He was lead singer for Geordie, his first band. In 1980 he'd join AC/DC, whose original singer Scott Bon had just died, becoming recognized as a great rock vocalist. Shortly beforehand I'd art directed and shot photos for Geordie's second album, *Don't Be Fooled by the Name.*

Andy Warhol, Mick Jagger, Lou Reed New York, 1976–1977

Top line: a) Andy and Mick—World Trade Centre, 1977. *b)* Andy and Lou—Launch party for Lou's album *Rock and Roll Heart* at One Fifth Avenue restaurant, 1976. *Second line:* Andy—Party at the apartment of Tom Forcade (second from left of Andy), founder of *High Times* magazine. *Third line:* Lou—With his dachshunds, The Baron and The Duke, 1976.

Iggy Pop and **Andrew Loog Oldham** New York, 1981

Shot at my Lexington Avenue studio at 32nd Street. I was in the middle of a session with Iggy when Andrew, who had been my New York friend since 1977, called and asked if he could drop by. Iggy was very keen to meet him. So Andrew came by and I snapped a few pix of them together.

Truman Capote and **Andy Warhol** New York, 1979

Shot at Andy's Factory on Union Square East. Cover shoot for *High Times* magazine. There was stuff everywhere, finding somewhere to set up was the trickiest part. They rented two Santa suits, but Truman decided not to wear his. Andy pointed at my feet. "Excuse me, I think you're standing on some of my canvases."

Ronnie Spector, Wayne County, The Ladybirds 1972–1975

Top line: Ronnie—The Rainbow Room at the Big Biba store, London, 1974. *Second line:* Wayne—On the basement stage at the Mercer Arts Centre, New York, 1972 (long before he changed sex and became Jayne). *Bottom line:* The Ladybirds—London, 1975. This glittery all-girl topless go-go four-piece band were based in Las Vegas, but they were from Denmark.

Mick Jagger, Rod Stewart, Ron Wood, Jeff Beck London, 1975

Shot in Portobello Road. A friend's party, where Ronnie, Mick, Jeff, and Rod showed up. The quartet gravitated towards a synthesizer in the top of the house, and started jamming—to the consternation of neighbors who called the police! The constabulary threatened to book the lads for "disorderly conduct," but I don't recall them actually doing it.

Ron Asheton London, 1972

Shot in the basement of the Fulham Road Rehearsal Studios. The original guitarist with The Stooges, who played bass guitar during their *Raw Power* period. It's sad that it took his death in 2009 for there to be such an outpouring of praise for his brilliance. He was voted #29 on *Rolling Stone*'s list of the greatest guitarists of all time.

Dead Boys Miami, 1977

Shot at a photo studio in Miami. Outtake from *We Have Come for Your Children* album cover session. The band were recording their second album at Criteria Studios and I was invited to shoot the cover. I had in mind *The Rolling Stones No. 2* album jacket, which the band loved. The shot used is pretty cool, but this one, shown here for the first time, is better.

Stiv Bators New York, 1981

Shot at my Lexington Avenue studio at 32nd Street. Outtake from *Rolling Stone* magazine session. After the dissolution of the Dead Boys, Stiv told me he'd formed The Lords of the New Church with Brian James from The Damned, and would I take some photos of them for *Rolling Stone.* Which of course I was happy to do; I took some doubles and solos. This shot is published here for the first time.

The Ramones New York, 1979

Shot at my studio on Lexington Avenue. Outtake from *End of the Century* cover session. The album was produced by Phil Spector. They were not a comfortable band to shoot, you could feel the tensions among them. They'd rejected two photo sessions and didn't have much budget left but were desperate. "They don't have much patience with photographers," their manager, Danny Fields, told me.

New York Dolls New York, 2007

Shot at Studio Industria. Outtake from *Interview* magazine session. I hadn't photographed the Dolls since I last saw them perform at the Big Biba store in London, in October 1973. Of course only two members of the original band were present, David and Sylvain Sylvain, the other original members having died.

Sex Pistols London, 1976 & 1977

Top: Shot at 100 Club, 1976. The mania truly surged with their first single "Anarchy in the UK" in November 1976. *Bottom: Shot at Denmark Street, 1977.* Outtake from *Stern* magazine session. Johnny explained: "Glen Matlock has just left the band. Malcolm says he's sorry he forgot to tell you . . . but nobody in Germany knows what we look like. One of the lads will fill in, just hide his face."

Steve Marriott London, 1974

Shot at Charlton Athletic Football Club. With his band Humble Pie—Lou Reed and The Who were also on the bill. I met Steve in a recording studio in 1991, introduced by Andrew Loog Oldham. He seemed very animated and positive that night and was working on some new recordings he'd made with Peter Frampton. Two weeks later he died in a fire at his home in the UK.

Talking Heads New York, 1977

Shot at Photographics Unlimited Studio on 21st Street. Outtake from *Talking Heads:77* album session. The front cover was a brilliant orange with only the title. The photos were used on the back and inside of the package, and for publicity. Not really a "punk" band, they were very clean-shaven, cooperative, and polite—although they did come into the public eye first at CBGB's.

Johnny Thunders New York, 1978

Shot at the Great Gildersleeves Club on The Bowery. Johnny with his band The Heartbreakers. Just down the road from CBGB's, the club was just as "seedy and sleazy" although it never acquired the same cachet. I last saw Johnny a week before his death. He discussed his ongoing dispute with Dee Dee Ramone over who wrote "Chinese Rocks." It's an issue that's still the subject of rock lore.

Patti Smith New York, 1976

Shot at The Bottom Line at the time of the release of Radio Ethiopia. I'd seen her at The Roundhouse in London, her first UK gig, and loved the anarchic lunacy of her performance. Plus she was strikingly photogenic. A few years ago at a party at Michael Stipe's apartment, she told me she didn't really like to be photographed, although she herself loved to take photos.

Dave Grohl Manchester, 2006

Shot at Old Trafford Cricket Ground. I'd never seen the Foo Fighters play before, so I wasn't quite ready for such a powerful performance. Certainly one of the best shows I'd seen in recent years. One of the sponsors was XFM Radio, who had flown me in, partly to tape some shows for the weekly DJ programme I was doing for them, and partly to shoot the two-day festival.

David Johansen New York, 1972

Shot at the Mercer Arts Centre. The Mercer was a shrine to New York's early glam/punk scene. I went with Bowie, his wife Angie, Mick Ronson, and my first wife Sheila. We hung out with Johansen and the rest of the New York Dolls after the gig. Johnny Thunders told me: "We all wanna make it so bad we'd sell our mothers . . . no, so bad we'd sell your mothers."

Johnny Rotten London, 1977

Shot in Denmark Street. Outtake from *Stern* magazine session. The Sex Pistols' obnoxious attitude was already news in the UK, and the word was creeping into Europe. Another photo of Johnny from the session would be the band's first ever national US magazine cover, in November '77 for *High Times*, for whom I shot several covers in the late 1970s.

Wendy O Williams New York, 1981

Shot at Bonds Casino, Times Square. It was after the legendary Clash gig there in May 1981. It was the loudest show I've ever attended. Wendy was a great performer, and the Plasmatics were visually very striking. But the music was totally forgettable. I hung out with her one night and in spite of her extrovert act, she seemed very subdued and sensitive. Tragically she shot herself in the head in 1998.

Dave Grohl Manchester, 2006

Shot at Old Trafford cricket ground. This was the same day. I had an all-access photo pass, so I was able to go backstage before the Foo Fighters hit the stage and take photos, including this one of Dave in full extrovert mode. Also on the festival bill were The Strokes and Richard Ashcroft, among others.

Thurston Moore and **Kim Gordon**
New York, 2005

Shot in their loft on Lafayette Street. Outtake from *Uncut* magazine feature session. The husband and wife duo from the critically acclaimed band Sonic Youth. They were getting ready to leave town that day, but kindly delayed their departure so that we could do the session. I used daylight through one of the big windows available.

Bob Geldof London, 2006

Shot at the O2 Wireless Festival, Hyde Park. We were both heading for the stage to watch The Raconteurs, and stopped and chatted. He wondered if I had any photos from the early 1980s Boomtown Rats show at the Ritz, New York, which I hadn't, though I'd seen the concert. I also mentioned that I've sometimes been mistaken for him . . . something to do with unruly hair, long jawline, and downbeat attire!

Andrew Loog Oldham and **Lou Adler**
New York, 1983

Shot in CBS Recording Studio, 33rd Street. Andrew and Lou were producing a performance of Marc Shaiman's musical *Dementos: Street People.* Lou was a longtime friend of Andrew, who once described him to me as "my L.A. godfather." It was a one-off moment where their focus is synchronized, they look like brothers, and they're both holding Italian ices!

The Gossip San Diego, 2009

Shot at the W Hotel. Outtake from W Hotels and Sony Records promotional session. They'd played San Francisco the previous evening, and had driven down overnight—and were pretty drunk! So they arrived late for the session, but apologized, and singer Beth Ditto was very playful. Even with little time I got great results. Later Beth and I did a bunch of flirty photos together on the red carpet!

Kasabian New York, 2006

Shot at Milk Studios. Outtake from *Playboy*'s Music Issue, 2007 session. One of the best of the new Brit rock bands, I had shot them a year earlier. They already knew my sense of humor so it was an easy shoot, and although it was basically a fashion session, I shot a series of close-up portraits toward the end, including this one.

Tony Wilson Manchester, 2006

Shot in the parking lot of XFM Radio. Like myself a graduate of Cambridge University, Tony was the legendary impresario who started Factory Records and The Hacienda Club in Manchester in the early 80s. I'd just done an interview for his radio show but I hadn't reckoned with his Weimaraner dog who was running about with Tony in hot pursuit. Tony died of cancer in 2007, a great loss.

Adam Green New York, 2008

Shot at the Milk Gallery. Outtake from "Nobody Was Thirsty" charity promotional session. I first photographed him in 2003 with the anti-folk duo Moldy Peaches, with Kimya Dawson. A man of eclectic tastes, he's also a fine visual artist, and in our sessions he loves to throw in the unexpected: as in this shot where he persuaded the makeup artist to render a black eye for him!

Jesse Hughes and **Josh Homme**
Los Angeles, 2006

Shot at Henry Fonda Theatre, Hollywood Blvd. Outtake from Ray-Ban promotional session. Jesse's band The Eagles of Death Metal were playing, and Josh (of The Queens of the Stone Age) was supporting his best friend onstage. It was like photographing brothers. The shot was outside the theatre, the background view is a reflection in one of the windows.

Bono and **Lady Gaga** New York, 2009

Shot at The Spotted Pig, West 11th Street. The afterparty for the concert *Gavin Friday and Friends* at Carnegie Hall, a special 50th birthday event for Bono's boyhood friend Gavin of the cult band The Virgin Prunes. The "friends" included all of U2, Rufus Wainwright, Lou Reed, Courtney Love, Flo & Eddie, Laurie Anderson, Shane MacGowan, and Lady Gaga, and the reconstituted Prunes themselves.

James Murphy New York, 2006

Shot in a record store in the West Village. Outtake from Ray-Ban promotional session. This was a tiny record store which has now closed. Originally a DJ, with his LCD Soundsystem project, James is basically a producer who also has a live band. His music has been described as "dance-punk," and I've been a fan since he released the single "Losing My Edge" in 2002.

Michael Pitt New York, 2008

Shot at Splashlight Studios. Outtake from *City* magazine session. I knew him from his movie role in *Hedwig and the Angry Inch*, but his finest part was based on Kurt Cobain in Gus Van Sant's *Last Days.* He feels like a real rock 'n' roller, a very good musician and singer. He came up with the idea of dipping his fingers in black oil to create an enigmatic portrait.

Syd Barrett London, 1969

Shot at Wetherby Mansions, Earls Court. Outtake from *The Madcap Laughs* album sessions. Syd had just woken and was still in his underpants, his bed was a mattress in the middle of the floor. These were hippie days! Remastering this shot, first published here in this form, I rescanned the original, and had my technician Lucky bring out the information of the view outside the windows embedded in the chrome.

Syd Barrett London, 1969

Shot at Wetherby Mansions, Earls Court. Top: I sent Syd's sister, Rosemary, this print. She had seen it in my book *Psychedelic Renegades*. She said: "It shows the cheeky, funny charismatic boy he was. I love it!" *Bottom:* Syd's other face, my "To Be or Not to Be" image. He seems to be mulling the existential dilemma he was caught in: to carry on playing or to withdraw. He chose the latter course.

Syd Barrett Cambridge, 1971

Shot in the basement of his mother's house in Cambridge. That day I conducted Syd's final interview, for *Rolling Stone*, which contains the oft-quoted statements, "I'm full of dust and guitars" and "I've got a very irregular head. And I'm not anything that you think I am anyway." The only available light source was a naked lightbulb. They're very grainy and dramatic, and have been rarely seen.

Lou Reed New York, 2003

Shot at the Pastis Bar/Restaurant, 9th Avenue and 12th Street. Outtake from *Uncut* magazine session. It was my first session with Lou in many years, and I was glad to have him in front of my lens again. He said he felt the same. In the 1970s Lou was one of my favorite subjects.

Debbie Harry New York, 2003

Shot at the Eagle's Nest Studio. Outtake from *Rebel* magazine session. Styled by Stella Zotis, who also did the makeup, and hair by Gerald DeCock. The most photogenic lady to be produced by rock 'n' roll, it's been a privilege to photograph her over the years. Even in more recent years she's still a beautiful subject, as this photo bears witness.

Iggy Pop Miami, 2007

Shot at a photo studio in Miami. Outtake from *Playboy* Music Issue session. I was buzzed shooting Iggy again, and rattled off nearly 1000 frames. We discussed our *Raw Power* sessions from long ago, and he reminded me they couldn't give the album away in 1973—"Three months after its release, I found a copy in a 50-cent bin!" But times change, and now the "Godfather of Punk" gets overwhelming respect.

David Bowie New York, 2002

Shot at Milk Studios. Outtake from *V* magazine session. We shot for three hours and David seemed to have a great time. He brought a load of CDs and played DJ. The green screens echo David's Ziggy image, and of course he's holding a set of metal balls! Plus he still looks so terrific after such an intense life, a superbly photogenic man.

David Bowie New York, 2002

Shot at Milk Studios. The same session, David's wearing my black scarf. There's a photo of Picasso by Irving Penn, his face half hidden by a scarf, and I thought a *hommage* appropriate. Of course David has no hat, and his right hand is visible, plus I got the lighting perfectly placed to produce a glint in his eye. It's probably my favorite of any I've taken of David.

Mick Rock and **Kate Moss**
New York, 2002
Shot at Milk Studios.

Andrew Loog Oldham
New York, 2009

Shot at Lombardy Hotel, 56th Street and Park Avenue. Andrew was in town for the funeral of Allen Klein which we both attended to pay our deep respects. We hooked up again shortly afterwards and I did a really fun interview with Andrew for his radio programme *Conversations with Andrew Loog Oldham.*

Mick Rock New York, 2005

Moonage Daydream 1994

Photocollage of David Bowie (original photo taken 1973). I have created many photocollages over the years (I call them "Ripart") including several of David.

"No work of art ever puts forward views. Views belong to people who are not artists."

Oscar Wilde

AFTERWORD

If writing is thinking on paper, then Mick Rock thinks on film, and our rock 'n' roll collective is the better for his thoughts. I met Mick Rock late in the 1970s, which was the beginning of the end of the 1960s for the many fortunate folk who had avoided Altamont and the all, and the West Coast denim drabness and madness that mellowed and Manson'd up our lives. Apart from Bowie, Marc Bolan, Chinn & Chapman, and what was left on the street, England had fallen into long play malaise with the big brands either breaking up, faking up, or taxing out.

I was already living in New York. I had met my wife, the Colombian actress Esther Farfan, in London in 1974 at the Saville Theatre during the Willy Russell play *John, Paul, George, Ringo and Bert*. I was fascinated by her neck and am still getting accustomed to her face that makes my day begin. We had settled up in New York just as Studio 54 opened and reigned and CBGB's punked and New Waved as New York entered its own form of the 1960s with music, fashion, and highlife everywhere. It was the place to be. John Lennon agreed.

The times were so very good that I know Mick will forgive me for forgetting exactly where it was we met, but rest assured it was some enchanted evening. Most photographers are well-teched pedestrians, and that alas leads to some resentment towards the subject at hand—the moment, the movement, the star. Mick Rock is a rock 'n' roll star, and a lovely fellow to boot, as thin, railed on previous occasion, charismatic, and outrageous as any rocker he has snapped. At this he would go coy and protest he's just a normal boy. He is as accomplished, interesting—interested as any diva I have met.

When we first met in helter shelter New York, I thought he was about to devour me. His need to know about what makes everything and everybody tick is engaging, a part of Mick and a part of his art of being Mick; he does not miss a beat and he does not miss a click. He has the ability to channel his subjects because he meets them on a level playing field. To be in a room or on the street rabbiting with him about life and the folks we have both been privileged to work with is a present time joy. His enthusiasm is in the work and the life now.

Time has moved on since those 1960s and 1970s, and so has Mick. Today when bands and artists need more than ever the support and respect that record companies used to give them, whilst taking the rest away, it has become tough out there for an artist to develop and not blow their load getting to first base. Mick Rock was part of that development. He worked with Iggy, Bowie, Lou Reed, Queen, and many others at pivotal moments in their careers. Mick Rock was as happy in a room with George Hurrell, Andy Warhol, Johnny Rotten, or Nico, and they were all happy to work and hang with him. And, of course, he's still clicking and hanging today, as this book bears witness, with the likes of The Killers, Snoop Dogg, Lady Gaga, Maxwell, Rufus Wainwright, Pete Yorn, etc.

Mick and I first worked together with a Texas band I was recording, The Werewolves. We made videos with the band years before there was an MTV, as in there was no place to show our video. That did not concern us in the slightest. We filmed in the Chelsea Hotel and recreated a scene from *Whatever Happened to Baby Jane?* with the guitarist doing his solo as Bette Davis. We had fun getting it done, and there was so much more.

In a profile on Mr. Cool—Miles Davis—by the erudite, edutaining Kenneth Tynan, a journalist in the 1960s, Tynan congratulates Mr. Davis on his first recording, made in 1948. The jazz legend asks the journo as to when he first heard the recording, and he answers as to having heard it in the past year. "Man," said Miles, with a broad emphatic grin, "You should have heard it in 1948!" Some fellas learn three chords to impress the ladies. Mick Rock picked up a camera and captured a world. Yours, mine, and theirs. The joy of his work and this book is that you can see all the moments now.

Mick Rock—a brighter light in a very dark room.

Andrew Loog Oldham

> **"There are no accidents. Anything that comes to you, you have put out beams for it."** Yogi Bhajan

Kabuki, New York 2008

My sincerest gratitude to:

Colin Webb of Palazzo Editions for his belief in this project and his relentless shepherding of it through the highways and byways; Adrian Cross for his enduring patience and his brilliant design sense; Steve Mockus and the team at Chronicle Books for their enthusiasm and commitment; Liz Vap for her endless support, loyalty, and counsel; Allen Klein, Andrew Loog Oldham, and Iris Keitel for saving my life; Tom Stoppard for his charming foreword; Andrew Loog Oldham for his delightful afterword; Dean Holtermann for his video eye and being a true friend; David Bowie for being such a great front cover image.

My enduring thanks to:

Pati Rock, Nathalie Rock, Joan Rock, Mike Evans, Pam Webb, John Varvatos, Annie Toglia, Catherine Alexander, Razor, Kabuki, Coco, Richard Lasdon, Lisa Raden, Raj Prem, Nestor Savas, Yujan Shao, Howard Weintraub, Steve Kalalian, Sal Scamardo, Ernie Thormahlen, John Serubo, Mazdack Rassi, Michael Chambers, Peter Blachley and all at the Morrison Hotel Galleries, Theron Kabrich of SFAE, Carlos Becil, Jonathan Sabatini, Jason Pomeranc, Julie Panebianco, Nur Khan, Errol Kolosine, Ioannis, Prince Peter, Warwick Stone, Marlon Richards, Cody Smyth, Jacqui Meyer, Joseph DeAcetis, Jennifer Ryan Jones, Karl Bridgeman, Benji Caillot, Carol Ming, Paul Shoefield, Nick Davidson, Ted Mason, Chris Polinsky, Kevin Cann, Andrew Melchior, Chet and Angie Milia, Nick Roylance, Cathy Roylance, Mat Vlasic, Richard Kerris, Henry Wrenn Meleck, George Fleck, Gray Shealy, Jane Stuart, Mike Kelly, Jeffrey Gewirtz, Len Sealy, Donna Faircloth, Alexandra Kwiatkowski, Lyonel Tollemache, Angela McCluskey, Mandy Brooks, Kari Bauce, Dan Barton, Eddie Brannan, Kelly Cutrone, Jody Klein, Stacey Bendet Eisner, Alexis Laken, Mick Gochanour, Richie Rich, Thomas Dozol, Sue Stemp, Ann Jones, Johnny Kaps, Terry Fraser, Rupert Perry, Peter Palmer, Martin Klipp, Robby Elson, Tim Mohr, Aaron Zych, Theo Dorian, Elva Corrie, JesseMallin, Kari Bauce, Johnny T, Alexandra Baker, Scott Lipps, Angela Milia, Laura Milia, Donald Milia, Sioux Zimmerman, Asif Ahmed, Jennifer Howell and The Art of Elysium, Russell Young, Julie Ragolia, Bryan Rabin, Anthony McAndrew, Jessica Daly, Kerry Collins, Ken Friedman, Jay Bluestine, Jan Walaker, Craig Schlossberg, Lucky Singh, Sat Jivan Singh, Sat Jivan Kaur.

Bibliography

Mick Rock: A Photographic Record 1969–1980, published 1995
Moonage Daydream: Ziggy Stardust (with David Bowie), published 2002
Killer Queen (foreword by Brian May), published 2003
Picture This: Debbie Harry and Blondie (foreword by Debbie Harry), published 2004
Raw Power: Iggy & The Stooges (foreword by IggyPop) published 2005
Glam! An Eyewitness Account (foreword by David Bowie), published 2005
Rocky Horror (foreword by Richard O'Brien), published 2006
Psychedelic Renegades: Syd Barrett, published 2006
Tamashii: Mick Rock Meets Kanzaburo (Kabuki Theatre Photos), published 2007
Classic Queen, published 2007